W9-BKD-366

FIRST STEPS TO MASTERING THE JAPANESE WRITING SYSTEM

# Japanese
# HIRAGANA
# & KATAKANA
# for Beginners

The method that's helped thousands in
the U.S. and Japan learn Japanese successfully

**Timothy G. Stout**
Illustrated by Alexis Cowan

TUTTLE Publishing
Tokyo | Rutland, Vermont | Singapore

## The Tuttle Story: "Books to Span the East and West"

Many people are surprised to learn that the world's largest publisher of books on Asia had its humble beginnings in the tiny American state of Vermont. The company's founder, Charles E. Tuttle, belonged to a New England family steeped in publishing.

Immediately after WW II, Tuttle served in Tokyo under General Douglas MacArthur and was tasked with reviving the Japanese publishing industry. He later founded the Charles E. Tuttle Publishing Company, which thrives today as one of the world's leading independent publishers.

Though a westerner, Tuttle was hugely instrumental in bringing a knowledge of Japan and Asia to a world hungry for information about the East. By the time of his death in 1993, Tuttle had published over 6,000 books on Asian culture, history and art—a legacy honored by the Japanese emperor with the "Order of the Sacred Treasure," the highest tribute Japan can bestow upon a non-Japanese.

With a backlist of 1,500 titles, Tuttle Publishing is more active today than at any time in its past—inspired by Charles Tuttle's core mission to publish fine books to span the East and West and provide a greater understanding of each.

Published by Tuttle Publishing, an imprint of Periplus Editions (HK) Ltd.

**www.tuttlepublishing.com**

Copyright © 2011 by Periplus Editions (HK) Ltd.

ISBN 978-4-8053-1144-8

**Distributed by**

**North America, Latin America & Europe**
Tuttle Publishing
364 Innovation Drive, North Clarendon, VT 05759-9436 U.S.A.
Tel: 1 (802) 773-8930; Fax: 1 (802) 773-6993
info@tuttlepublishing.com   www.tuttlepublishing.com

**Japan**
Tuttle Publishing
Yaekari Building, 3rd Floor, 5-4-12 Osaki, Shinagawa-ku, Tokyo 141 0032
Tel: (81) 3 5437-0171; Fax: (81) 3 5437-0755
sales@tuttle.co.jp   www.tuttle.co.jp

**Asia Pacific**
Berkeley Books Pte. Ltd.
61 Tai Seng Avenue #02-12, Singapore 534167
Tel: (65) 6280-1330; Fax: (65) 6280-6290
inquiries@periplus.com.sg   www.periplus.com

17 16 15 14      10 9 8 7 6      1404MP

Printed in Singapore

# CONTENTS

Introduction...................................................................................5

## — HIRAGANA —

**SECTION ONE**
The Basic 46 Hiragana Characters ................................13
Reading Practice 1: あ ～ そ ....................................29
Reading Practice 2: た ～ ほ ....................................45
Reading Practice 3: ま ～ ん ....................................62

**SECTION TWO**
Hiragana Usage Rules..............................................63

**Rule 1:** Tenten and Maru ........................................64
**Reading Practice 4:** Tenten and Maru ........................71

**Rule 2:** Combined Characters ..................................71
**Reading Practice 5:** Combined Characters ..................77

**Rule 3:** Small "tsu" ..............................................78
**Reading Practice 6:** Small "tsu" ..............................79

**Rule 4: Long Vowels** ..............................................79
**Reading Practice 7:** Long Vowels ............................80

**Rule 5:** Sentence Particles "wa," "e" and "o" ............81
**Reading Practice 8:** Particles "wa," "e" and "o" ..........83

**SECTION THREE**
Reading and Writing Practice....................................84
Answers .............................................................99

## — KATAKANA —

**SECTION FOUR**
**The Basic 46 Katakana Characters**......................................................**100**
**Reading Practice 1:** ア ～ ソ ..........................................................**116**
**Reading Practice 2:** タ ～ ホ............................................................**132**
**Reading Practice 3:** マ ～ ン............................................................**149**

**SECTION FIVE**
**Katakana Usage Rules** ....................................................................**150**

**Rule 1:** Tenten and Maru ..............................................................**150**
**Reading Practice 4:** Tenten and Maru ..............................................**156**

**Rule 2:** Combined Characters ........................................................**157**
**Reading Practice 5:** Combined Characters ........................................**163**

**Rule 3:** Small "tsu" ....................................................................**163**
**Reading Practice 6:** Small "tsu" ....................................................**165**

**Rule 4:** Additional Combined Characters ........................................**165**
**Reading Practice 7:** Additional Combined Characters ..........................**172**

**SECTION SIX**
**Reading and Writing Practice**........................................................**173**
**Answers** ....................................................................................**187**

**Flash Card Practice Activities** ........................................................**191**

**Acknowledgments** ......................................................................**192**

# Introduction

You probably picked up this book because you are interested in the best way to learn hiragana and katakana. If so, you came to the right place. The methods in this book have helped thousands of students in the United States and Japan to successfully learn both, and they can help you too.

This book makes learning hiragana and katakana fast and effective by using clear explanations and examples and lots of fun exercises. It also features memorable picture mnemonics like the one below. Picture mnemonics enhance memory by associating the shape and sound of each character with pictures and English words already familiar to you. For example, the hiragana character "**mo**" as in "**mo**re" looks like a fishhook intersected by two lines, leading to the idea that "you can catch **mo**re fish with **mo**re bait."

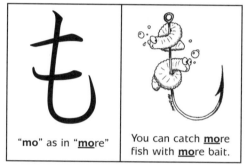

| "mo" as in "<u>mo</u>re" | You can catch <u>mo</u>re fish with <u>mo</u>re bait. |

Katakana and hiragana characters—together called **kana**—are the two sets of 46 phonetic characters used in Japanese. An average, diligent student can learn to read the basic 46 hiragana and 46 katakana characters in a few hours, and with persistence can learn to write them in a few days. If you study for thirty minutes a day, in a few short weeks you will be a confident reader and writer of hiragana and katakana.

## How to Use This Book

This introduction gives you basic information about the characters: where they came from, how to pronounce and write them, and even how to write your name.

Both hiragana and katakana are essential to basic Japanese proficiency, but normally hiragana is learned first. In Section One you will learn the basic 46 hiragana characters, and how to write some simple words. Section Two introduces the usage rules that will allow you to write all of the sounds of Japanese and gives you more opportunities for practice. Section Three strengthens your hiragana skills through a wide range of exercises designed to both increase your knowledge of the Japanese language and reinforce your newly acquired writing skills. Then in Sections Four, Five and Six you will follow the very same process to master the katakana characters.

At the end of the book you will find a list of suggested flash card activities. Since it is easier to learn to recognize hiragana and katakana than to write them, you may want to begin with the flash cards, printing them from the CD-ROM and reviewing them often. As you learn to recognize the characters, you will find it much easier to write them. Whether you begin with the writing sections or the flash cards, you will get the most out of this book by doing all the activities.

# An Overview of the Japanese Writing System

Japanese uses four types of scripts: hiragana, katakana, kanji and romaji.

- **Hiragana** is a cursive set of 46 phonetic characters that express all of the sounds of Japanese. Hiragana is used mainly for writing the grammatical parts of sentences and native Japanese words for which there are no kanji.
- **Katakana** is an angular set of 46 phonetic characters, generally used for writing foreign words and for showing emphasis.
- **Kanji** are characters of ancient Chinese origin that represent ideas and sounds, and they are used for most nouns, verbs and other "content" words. There are 2,131 "common use" kanji that school children must learn by ninth grade.
- **Romaji** are roman (Latin) letters used to write Japanese; you must already know romaji since you are reading this. Romaji is used in textbooks and dictionaries for foreigners learning Japanese (and for Japanese people learning western languages) but its use in day-to-day writing is somewhat limited to things like company names and acronyms.

| ひらがな<br>**Hiragana** | カタカナ<br>**Katakana** | 漢字<br>**Kanji** | **Romaji** |
|---|---|---|---|

Don't be too intimidated by the number and seeming complexity of Japanese characters. Japan's 99 percent literacy rate should allay any fears that learning Japanese is impossible. Compared to kanji, kana characters are not complex; each one only has between one and four strokes. Each set of kana has 46 characters, compared to the English alphabet which has 52 letters (26 upper case and 26 lower case). Although kana characters have a few more overall strokes than the letters of the alphabet, kana have a consistent one-to-one relationship between character and sound. By contrast more than half of the English alphabet letters have multiple pronunciations, and seemingly endless exceptions. Anyone who has learned the complexities of English spelling can succeed at learning kana. So, although learning hiragana and katakana may at first seem to be a Sumo-sized task, with the right training and practice you can do it! Before you know it you'll be a kana champion!

Don't rely on romaji. Foreigners learning Japanese sometimes rely on romaji, never learning to read and write. While it is possible to become quite proficient in speaking Japanese using only romaji, you will not be truly literate. Get comfortable using hiragana. When you buy a dictionary make sure it is written in hiragana, not romaji. When you write in Japanese use hiragana and katakana and kanji characters as you learn them.

# How to Pronounce Hiragana and Katakana

Hiragana and katakana are pronounced the same way. The first five characters are the five Japanese vowels. Japanese vowels are short and clipped compared to English vowels. (All of the examples in this book use Standard American English pronunciation).

| | |
|---|---|
| a | as in father |
| i | as in easy |
| u | as in you |
| e | as in red |
| o | as in oak |

The rest of the characters are consonant-vowel combinations, with the consonant always coming first (e.g., "ka," "ki," "ku," "ke" and "ko"). The one exception is the single consonant syllable "n" that is pronounced by touching the back of the tongue to the roof of the mouth, as in "ink" and "sing." Many Japanese consonants are commonly found in English and are easy to pronounce.

| | | | |
|---|---|---|---|
| k | as in coat | g | as in goat (voiced version of k) |
| s | as in Sue | z | as in zoo (voiced version of g) |
| t | as in tie | d | as in dye (voiced version of t) |
| n | as in no | | |
| h | as in house | | |
| p | as in pig | b | as in big (voiced version of p) |
| m | as in man | | |

Several Japanese consonants, however, are not commonly found in English and require special attention. One is the Japanese "r." In English "r" is pronounced by curling the tongue so the sides touch the upper teeth (not touching the tip of the tongue). In Japanese, "r" is pronounced by tapping the tongue against the ridge behind the upper teeth, as in "paddle" and "ladder," sounding like a combination of "l" and "d"; it is not a rolling trill as in Spanish. "tsu" is pronounced as in "tsunami" and "cat's whiskers." "fu" is pronounced without touching the upper teeth and lower lip. It almost sounds like "who" and "hooting owl," except the lips are more pursed and air escapes more quickly.

The special consonant "y" as in "yarn" is paired with the vowels "a," "u" and "o" to make the syllables "ya," "yu" and "yo." This consonant is special because Japanese uses it extensively in combination with all of the other consonants to form additional syllables, such as "kya," "kyu" and "kyo." In order to accommodate more foreign syllables, many more character combinations are used in katakana (see Section Five).

Although katakana tries to represent **gairaigo** ("loan words") as faithfully as possible, the words sound distinctly Japanese. In 1991 the Japanese government updated the official guidelines for writing **gairaigo**. The guidelines included 33 more combined characters for writing foreign words. These 33 combined characters are not the limit—the guidelines clearly state that other combinations can be made as needed. Still, all syllables must conform to the basics of Japanese phonology (see Section Two).

## How to Write Hiragana

Hiragana is the first writing system that Japanese children learn. It is not uncommon for a four-year-old to be able to fluently read children's books and the like because of hiragana's simple one-to-one correspondence between characters and sounds. Hiragana can easily be used to write any word or phrase, and even adults will sometimes substitute hiragana for difficult or uncommon kanji characters.

According to the U.S. Foreign Service Institute, it takes approximately 1,300 hours to acquire advanced Japanese proficiency, but much less time is required for basic proficiency. Hiragana is a great place to begin. The immediate benefits of learning hiragana include improving your pronunciation and gaining access to hundreds of dictionaries, textbooks, and other learning and enrichment materials written with hiragana. Plus, all of the writing skills of hiragana are transferable to learning katakana and kanji, making them easier to learn.

There are various styles used to write hiragana, but this book only uses the most standard **kyōkashotai** or "schoolbook" style. Hiragana characters are composed of three types of strokes: "stops," "jumps" and "brushes." With a stop, the pencil must come to a stop before it is removed from the paper. Jumps are written by removing the pencil from the paper as it moves to the next stroke. With a brush, the pencil is slowly removed from the paper as the stroke is written, giving it a tapered, sweeping appearance. In the example below, the character "ke" as in "**Ke**vin" is written with all three types of strokes. The first stroke is a jump, the second is a stop, and the third is a brush.

Writing the correct stroke types in the correct order is important for forming balanced, legible characters. With practice you will get the hang of it. You can make your characters look more authentic by slightly tilting left-to-right strokes, as in stroke two in "**ke**" (see above), rather than writing them straight across. Character strokes are generally written from left to right and top to bottom. Try to center each character in an imaginary box, not too far to the left, right, top or bottom.

| Correct! | Wrong | Wrong | Wrong | Wrong |
|---|---|---|---|---|

Traditionally Japanese was written from top to bottom, progressing in columns from right to left across the page. Now it is also commonly written from left to write, as with English. All the hiragana in this book is written from left to right.

# How to Write Katakana

Katakana characters also are composed of the same three types of strokes we discussed above: "stops," "jumps" and "brushes." In the following example, the character "**o**" as in "**o**ak" is written with all three types of strokes. The first is a stop, the second a jump, and the third is a brush.

Compare the hiragana and katakana characters below. Hiragana characters are curved and looping, but katakana characters are straight and angled. Katakana also has fewer "jumps" and more "stops" and "brushes."

| a | i | ka | ki | sa | shi | ta | chi |
|---|---|----|----|----|-----|----|----|
| あ | い | か | き | さ | し | た | ち |
| ア | イ | カ | キ | サ | シ | タ | チ |

Some hiragana and katakana characters look alike, like "**ka**" and "**ki**." The picture mnemonics for these katakana characters are the same as the hiragana characters—another good reason you should master hiragana first.

Writing the correct stroke type in the correct order is important for forming balanced, legible characters. With practice you will get the hang of it. You can make your characters look more authentic by slightly tilting left-to-right strokes, as in stroke one in "**o**" (see above), rather than writing them straight across. Character strokes are generally written from left to right and top to bottom. Try to center each character in the middle of an imaginary box, not too far to the top, bottom, left, or right.

| オ | オ | オ | オ | オ |
|---|---|---|---|---|
| Correct! | Wrong | Wrong | Wrong | Wrong |

# Writing Your Name in Japanese

Most beginning learners enjoy katakana because it is relatively simple to learn, and it is immediately useful. You write your name and your friends' names in katakana. You can guess many of the katakana words found in Japanese texts you read. Soon reading and writing katakana will become second nature, and all your hard work will begin to pay off.

Try to find your name in the "Names in Katakana" lists provided on the CD-ROM. Only one Japanese spelling is given for all of the names with the same pronunciation, such as Amy, Ami, Amie and Aimee. The names are listed under the most common spelling. If you don't see your name in the list and your name is a nickname, try looking for the formal version (i.e., "Richard" instead of "Rick"). If you still can't find your name, it may not be one of the most common. Never fear, you can ask your teacher or a Japanese friend for help. Any name can be written in Japanese. Practice writing your name in the spaces provided (don't worry if you leave some boxes unused).

# Where Hiragana and Katakana Came From

Although hiragana characters look like the picture mnemonics in this book, they did not originally come from pictures. Hiragana characters were developed based on simplified cursive-style kanji during the Heian Period (794-1185 AD). China, one of the great civilizations of the ancient world, had a huge influence on its Asian neighbors, including Japan. Kanji were first introduced to Japan around the 5th century AD.

The Japanese upper classes made a serious study of Chinese language, religion and government, and along with adopting new perspectives and practices, they adopted thousands of words and the kanji used to write them. The earliest official documents were written in Chinese, and for a long time Chinese was considered the language of the educated. Japanese also used kanji, however, to write poetry and prose in Japanese. This was problematic since spoken Japanese and Chinese were very different, but the Japanese overcame this challenge by giving kanji new Japanese pronunciations, and by using some kanji as phonetic characters to be able to express native Japanese words and grammatical elements in writing.

Kanji used as phonetic characters were called kana or "borrowed names," implying that using kanji to express only sounds was not the regular practice. The first set of kana, called **man'yōgana** (the line above the "o" indicates it is two syllables in length), was difficult to read because there were no one-to-one relationships between the characters and sounds, plus there were hundreds of them. **Man'yōgana** was also difficult to write because each phonetic syllable had to be written in kanji. To simplify things, two sets of kana called katakana and hiragana were developed over time. Katakana or "partial kana" as the name suggests was developed from parts of kanji (see the following example).

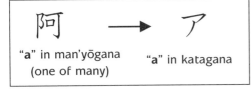

"a" in man'yōgana (one of many)     "a" in katagana

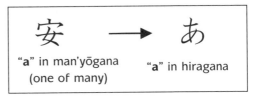

"a" in man'yōgana (one of many)     "a" in hiragana

Writing with katakana was originally limited to men, and used in official documents. Hiragana or "common kana" was developed based on simplified versions of entire kanji characters (see example above). It was used in informal writing, such as letters and diaries, and it was referred to as **onna-de** or "woman's hand."

Ironically, during the Heian period while the men were attempting to write in "superior" Chinese, some women who learned to write in hiragana produced the finest literature of the period. *The Tale of Genji* written 1,000 years ago by a court lady named Murasaki Shikibu is generally regarded as the world's first novel, and a classic. In time, men began using hiragana as well. Today Japanese is written with a mix of hiragana, katakana, kanji and romaji.

*The Tale of Genji* by Murasaki Shikibu
is over 1,000 pages in English translation.

History aside, you may be wondering why Japanese still has *two* sets of phonetic characters. The main reason is that it makes reading easier—katakana words stand out in a text, like a highlighter. When you see a katakana word, you immediately know it falls into one of six categories:
1. **Gairaigo** or "loan words"
2. Foreign place names and personal names
3. Onomatopoeia (sound symbolic words), like "buzz," "flip" and "bow wow," which are much more numerous in Japanese than in English
4. Emphasis words—normally written in hiragana or kanji, but that the writer wants to draw attention to
5. Dictionaries entries of **on-yomi** or the "Chinese readings" of kanji

6. Others, such as transcriptions of the Ainu language (indigenous to northern Japan), and some official documents of pre-modern Japan

**Gairaigo** or "loan words," such as **konpyūtā** (computer), **nyūsu** (news), and **resutoran** (restaurant), comprise the biggest category of katakana words, with tens of thousands in common use. Most **gairaigo** come from English, so even beginning learners can often correctly guess what a Japanese article is about just from scanning the text for **gairaigo**. Topics like sports, medicine, business, economy, technology, and science have numerous **gairaigo**.

*Japanese Hiragana and Katakana for Beginners* is the right place to begin your Japanese studies. As you learn kana you will be taking the first steps to mastering the Japanese writing system and its pronunciation. Taking Japanese in small steps will make it more manageable. As the Japanese proverb states, "Even dust piled up becomes a mountain." or in other words, little things add up!

ちりも積もれば山となる
**chiri mo tsumoreba yama to naru**
(Even dust piled up becomes a mountain.)

Good luck as you embark on this new journey. As you increase your understanding of the Japanese people and their wonderful culture and language you will find fresh encouragement to carry on. One step at a time you can do anything. So, let's get started. Turn the page and begin your journey.

# The Basic 46 Hiragana Characters

| | | | | |
|---|---|---|---|---|
| a あ ✓ | i い ✓ | u う ✓ | e え ✓ | o お ✓ |
| ka か ✓ | ki き ✓ | ku く ✓ | ke け | ko こ ✓ |
| sa さ ✓ | shi し ✓ | su す ✓ | se せ | so そ ✓ |
| ta た ✓ | chi ち ✓ | tsu つ ✓ | te て ✓ | to と ✓ |
| na な ✓ | ni に ✓ | nu ぬ | ne ね | no の |
| ha (wa)* は | hi ひ | fu ふ | he (e)* へ | ho ほ |
| ma ま | mi み | mu む | me め | mo も ✓ |
| ya や | | yu ゆ | | yo よ |
| ra ら | ri り | ru る | re れ | ro ろ |
| wa わ ✓ | | | | o** を |
| n ん ✓ | | | | |

* These characters are pronounced differently when they are used as grammatical particles.
** This character is only used as a grammatical particle. It is not used to write words.

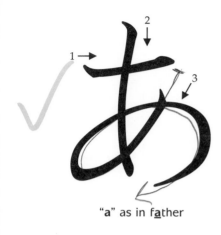

"a" as in f<u>a</u>ther

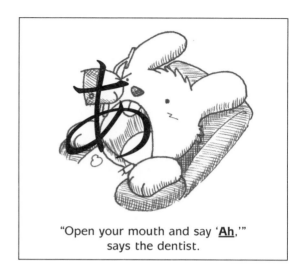

"Open your mouth and say '<u>Ah</u>,'" says the dentist.

**Writing Tip** "a" has three strokes: 1) a stop, 2) stop and 3) brush.

Trace these characters.

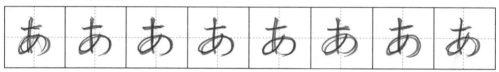

Write the character in the boxes below, and then circle the one you think is best.

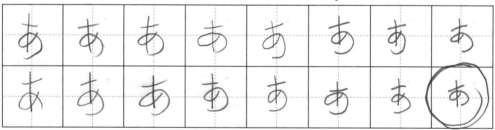

1. **a ka** (red)

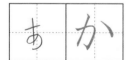

2. **a ri** (ant)

3. **a sa** (morning)

4. **a ki** (autumn)

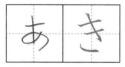

5. **a me** (rain; hard candy)

6. **a o** (blue)

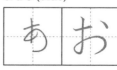

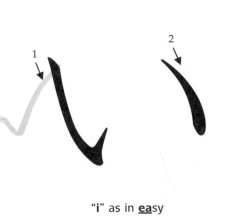

"i" as in **ea**sy

the two "i's" in Hawa**ii**

**Writing Tip** "i" has two strokes: 1) a jump and 2) stop.

Trace these characters.

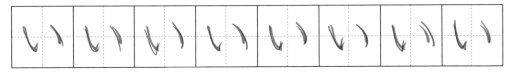

Write the character in the boxes below, and then circle the one you think is best.

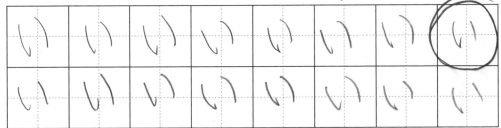

1. **i i** (good)

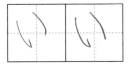

2. **i su** (chair)

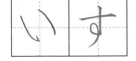

3. **ha i** (Yes!)

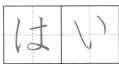

4. **o i shi i** (delicious)

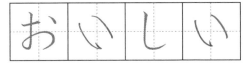

5. **i ka** (squid)

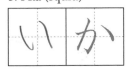

"**u**" as in y**ou**th

**<u>Ew</u>**! There's a bug on your ear!

**Writing Tip** "**u**" has two strokes: 1) a stop and 2) brush.

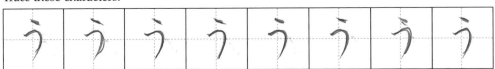

Trace these characters.

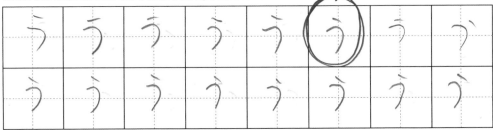

Write the character in the boxes below, and then circle the one you think is best.

1. **u chi** (home)

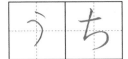

2. **u de** (arm)

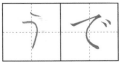

3. **u e** (up)

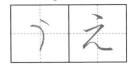

4. **u shi** (cow)

5. **u ma** (horse)

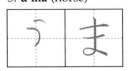

6. **u me** (plum)

"**e**" as in r**e**d

An **e**lf is hanging ornaments on a Christmas tree.

**Writing Tip** "e" has two strokes: 1) a jump and 2) zigzag stop.

Trace these characters.

Write the character in the boxes below, and then circle the one you think is best.

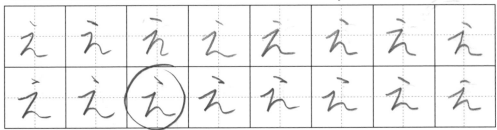

1. **e ki** (train station)

2. **ma e** (in front of)

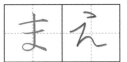

3. **e e** (yes – colloquial)

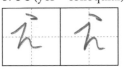

4. **e n** (yen)

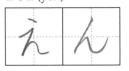

5. **ha e** (fly)

6. **e bi** (shrimp)

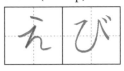

"o" as in <u>oa</u>k

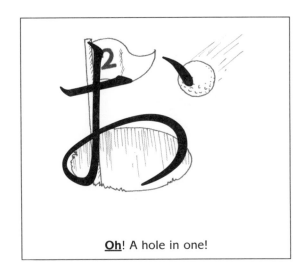

<u>Oh</u>! A hole in one!

**Writing Tip** "o" has three strokes: 1) a stop, 2) brush and 3) stop.

Trace these characters.

Write the character in the boxes below, and then circle the one you think is best.

1. **ka o** (face)

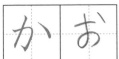

2. **o o ki i** (big)

3. **o ha shi** (chopsticks)

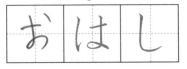

4. **o ka shi** (snacks)

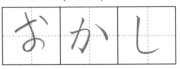

"**ka**" as in <u>ca</u>r

<u>Kah!</u> A crow cries as it flies to a tree on the top of a cliff.

**Writing Tip** "**ka**" has three strokes: 1) a jump, 2) stop and 3) stop.

Trace these characters.

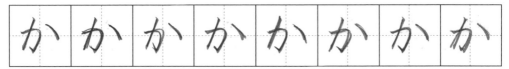

Write the character in the boxes below, and then circle the one you think is best.

1. **mi ka n** (mandarin orange)

2. **ka** (mosquito)  3. **ka sa** (umbrella)

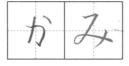

4. **chi ka** (basement)

5. **ka mi** (hair; paper; God)  6. **na ka** (inside)

"**ki**" as in **key**

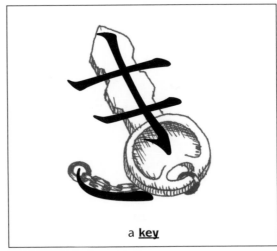

a **key**

**Writing Tip** "ki" has four strokes: 1) a stop, 2) stop, 3) jump and 4) stop.

Trace these characters.

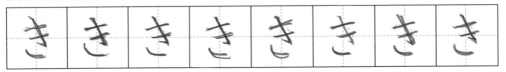

Write the character in the boxes below, and then circle the one you think is best.

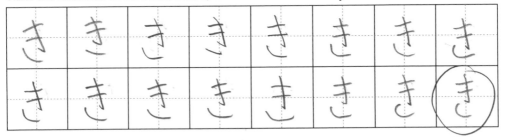

1. **yu ki** (snow)

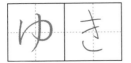

2. **ki ta** (north)

3. **e ki** (train station)

4. **te n ki** (weather)

5. **ki i ro** (yellow)

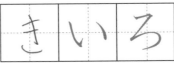

"**ku**" as in cuc**koo**

a cuc**koo**'s beak

**Writing Tip** "ku" has one stroke: a stop.

Trace these characters.

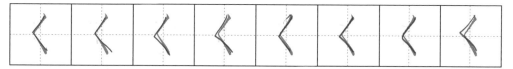

Write the character in the boxes below, and then circle the one you think is best.

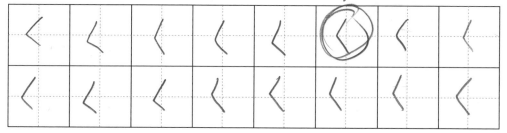

1. **ku ro** (black)

2. **ku chi** (mouth)

3. **ni ku** (meat)

4. **ku tsu** (shoe)

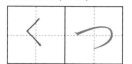

5. **ku ma** (bear)

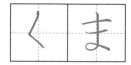

6. **ku mo** (spider; cloud)

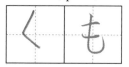

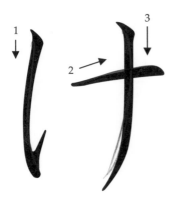

"ke" as in **Ke**vin

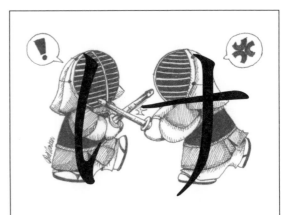

**Ke**ndo is a traditional Japanese sport using wooden swords.

**Writing Tip** "ke" has three strokes: 1) a jump, 2) stop and 3) brush.

Trace these characters.

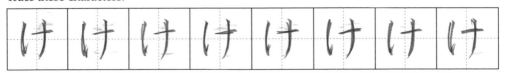

Write the character in the boxes below, and then circle the one you think is best.

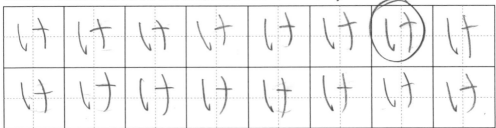

1. **ta ke** (bamboo)

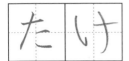

2. **i ke** (pond)

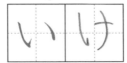

3. **ke su** (to erase)

4. **to ke i** (clock)

5. **ta su ke te** (Help!)

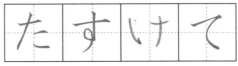

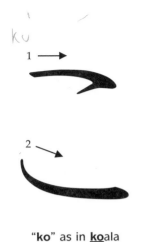

"ko" as in **ko**ala

A **ko**ala is climbing a tree.

**Writing Tip** "ko" has two strokes: 1) a jump and 2) stop.

Trace these characters.

Write the character in the boxes below, and then circle the one you think is best.

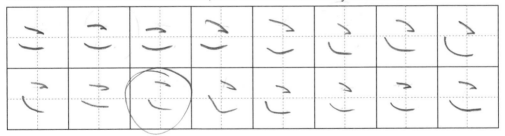

1. **ko re** (this)

2. **do ko** (where?)

3. **ko ko** (here)

4. **ko do mo** (child)

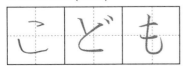

5. **i to ko** (cousin)

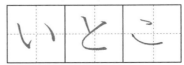

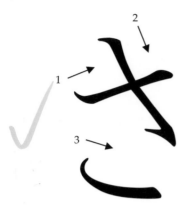

"**sa**" as in **sa**w

He **sa**w something that made him smile.

**Writing Tip** "**sa**" has three strokes: 1) a stop, 2) jump and 3) stop.

Trace these characters. 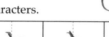 or

Write the character in the boxes below, and then circle the one you think is best.

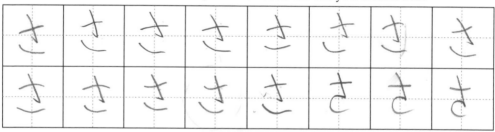

1. **sa mu i** (cold)

2. **ha sa mi** (scissors)

3. **sa n** (Mr./Mrs./Ms./Miss) 4. **sa n** (three)

5. **sa ru** (monkey)

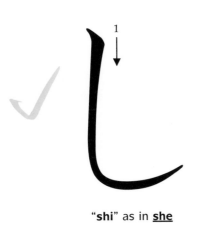

"**shi**" as in **she**

**She** has a ponytail.

**Writing Tip** "shi" has one stroke: a brush.

Trace these characters.

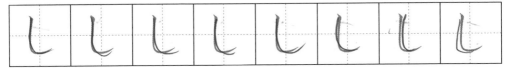

Write the character in the boxes below, and then circle the one you think is best.

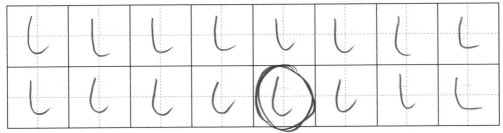

**1. shi ro** (white)

**2. a shi** (legs)

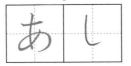

**3. shi o** (salt)

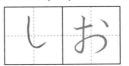

**4. mu shi** (insect)

**5. shi ka** (deer)

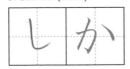

**6. na shi** (Asian pear)

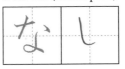

"**su**" as in **su**per

It's another perfect dive by **Su**per Diver.

**Writing Tip** "**su**" has two strokes: 1) a stop and 2) looping brush.

Trace these characters.

Write the character in the boxes below, and then circle the one you think is best.

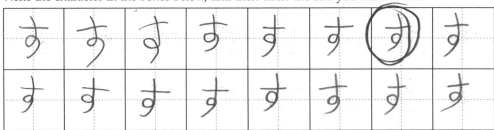

1. **su mō** (sumo)

2. **su** (vinegar)

3. **su shi** (sushi)

4. **ri su** (squirrel)

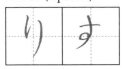

5. **su ki** (like – adjective)

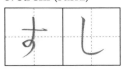

6. **su ru** (to do)

"**se**" as in <u>se</u>t

Mother <u>se</u>ts Baby on her lap.

**Writing Tip** "**se**" has three strokes: 1) a stop, 2) jump and 3) stop.

Trace these characters.

Write the character in the boxes below, and then circle the one you think is best.

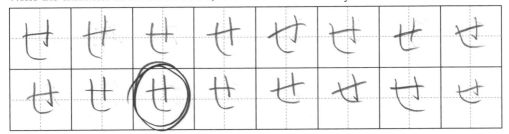

1. **se n se i** (teacher; doctor; dentist)

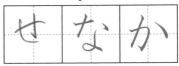

2. **se na ka** (a person's back)

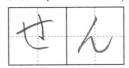

3. **se mi** (cicada)

4. **se ki** (cough; seat)

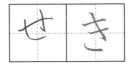

5. **se n** (one thousand)

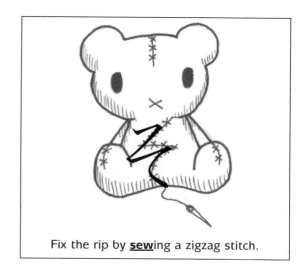

"**so**" as in **sew**ing machine

Fix the rip by **sew**ing a zigzag stitch.

**Writing Tip** "so" has one stroke: a zigzag stop.

Trace these characters.

Write the character in the boxes below, and then circle the one you think is best.

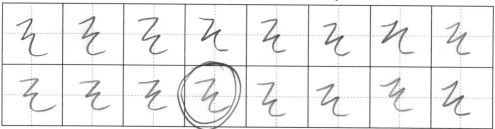

1. **so to** (outside)

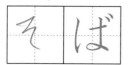

2. **so ko** (there)

3. **so re** (that)

4. **so ba** (buckwheat noodles)

5. **so ra** (sky)

6. **u so** (lie; false)

## READING PRACTICE 1: あ ～ そ

You should be able to read the words below now. Fold the page lengthwise (or cover it with your hand) so you can only see the hiragana words on the left hand side. Try reading them aloud and then check with the words on the right. Keep practicing until you can read them all. For an extra challenge try reading the Japanese and saying the English word before checking.

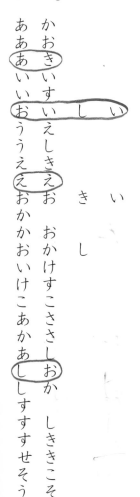

**a ka** (red)
**a o** (blue)
**a ki** (autumn)
**i i** (good)
**i su** (chair)
**o i shi i** (delicious)
**u e** (up, above)
**u shi** (cow)
**e ki** (train station)
**e e** (yes – colloquial)
**o o ki i** (big)
**ka** (mosquito)
**ka o** (face)
**o ka shi** (snacks)
**i ke** (pond)
**ke su** (to erase)
**ko ko** (here)
**a sa** (morning)
**ka sa** (umbrella)
**a shi** (leg; foot)
**shi o** (salt)
**shi ka** (deer)
**su** (vinegar)
**su shi** (sushi)
**su ki** (like – adjective)
**se ki** (cough; seat)
**so ko** (there)
**u so** (lie; false)

| Romaji pronunciation guide: | |
|---|---|
| *a* | as in **father** |
| *i* | as in **easy** |
| *u* | as in **you** |
| *e* | as in **red** |
| *o* | as in **oak** |

"**ta**" as in <u>ta</u>lk

"**t**" and "**a**" spell "<u>ta</u>"

**Writing Tip** "**ta**" has four strokes and all four are stops.

Trace these characters.

Write the character in the boxes below, and then circle the one you think is best.

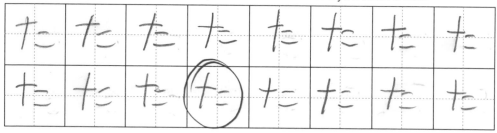

**1. a ta ma** (head)

**2. ta no shi i** (fun; enjoyable)

**3. i ta i** (Ouch!)

**4. ta ka i** (high; tall; expensive)

"chi" as in <u>chee</u>r

a <u>chee</u>rleader

**Writing Tip** "chi" has two strokes: 1) a stop and 2) brush.

Trace these characters.

Write the character in the boxes below, and then circle the one you think is best.

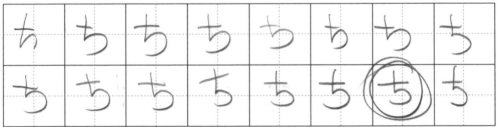

1. **i chi** (one)

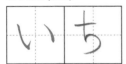

2. **u chi** (home; house)

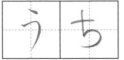

3. **ku chi** (mouth)

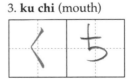

4. **mi chi** (road; path)

5. **shi chi** (seven)

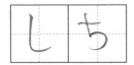

6. **ha chi** (eight; bee)

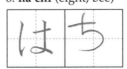

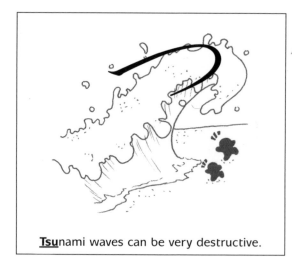

"**tsu**" as in **tsu**nami

**Tsu**nami waves can be very destructive.

**Writing Tip** "tsu" has one stroke: a brush.

Trace these characters.

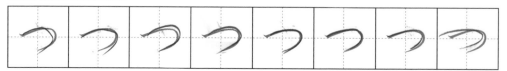

Write the character in the boxes below, and then circle the one you think is best.

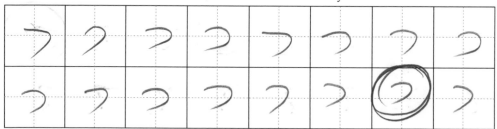

1. **a tsu i** (hot)

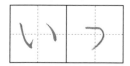

2. **tsu na mi** (tsunami wave)

3. **i tsu** (when)

4. **ku tsu** (shoes)

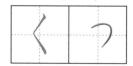

5. **tsu yo i** (strong)

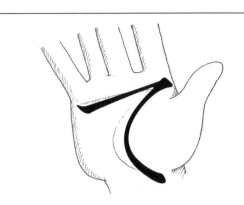

"**te**" as in <u>te</u>n

The shape of "**te**" is in the palm of your right hand, and the word for "hand" in Japanese is "**te**."

**Writing Tip** "**te**" has one stroke: a stop.

Trace these characters.

Write the character in the boxes below, and then circle the one you think is best.

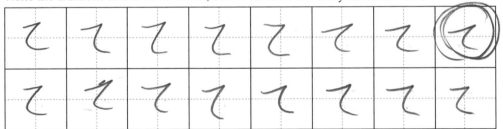

1. **te** (hand)  2. **ka ra te** (karate)

3. **su te ki** (lovely; cool; superb)

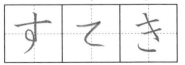

4. **chi ka te tsu** (subway)

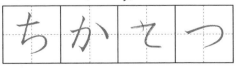

5. **te n ki** (weather)

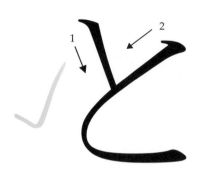

"**to**" as in <u>toe</u>

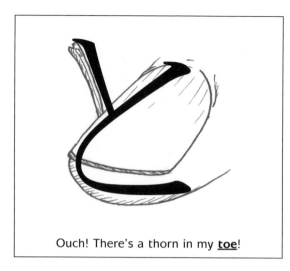

Ouch! There's a thorn in my <u>toe</u>!

**Writing Tip** "to" has two strokes and both are stops.

Trace these characters.

Write the character in the boxes below, and then circle the one you think is best.

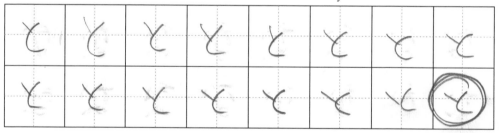

1. **to ra** (tiger)

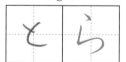

2. **to ri** (bird)

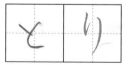

3. **hi to** (person)

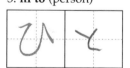

4. **so to** (outside)

5. **o to to i** (day before yesterday)

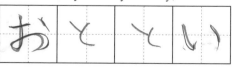

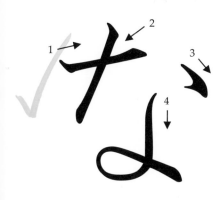

"**na**" as in to **gna**w

A beaver is **gna**wing on a tree.

**Writing Tip** "**na**" has four strokes: 1) a stop, 2) stop, 3) jump and 4) stop.

Trace these characters.

Write the character in the boxes below, and then circle the one you think is best.

1. **na tsu** (summer)

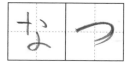

2. **na ni** (what)

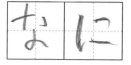

3. **na ka** (inside; middle)

4. **na ma e** (name)

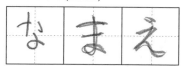

5. **mi n na** (all; everyone)

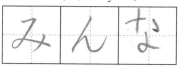

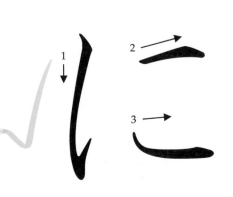

"ni" as in <u>knee</u>

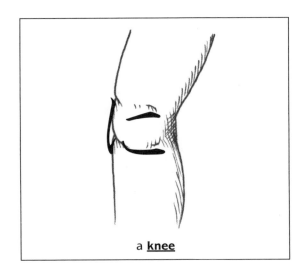

a <u>knee</u>

**Writing Tip** "ni" has three strokes: 1) a jump, 2) stop and 3) stop.

Trace these characters.

Write the character in the boxes below, and then circle the one you think is best.

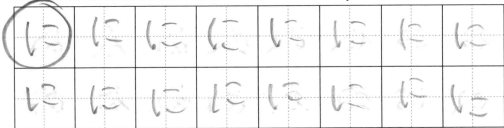

1. **ku ni** (country; nation)

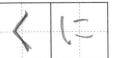

2. **ni ku** (meat)

3. **wa ni** (alligator)

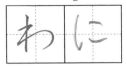

4. **ni ho n** (Japan)

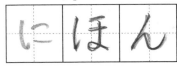

5. **ma i ni chi** (everyday)

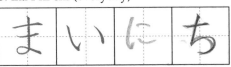

1

2

"**nu**" as in **ne**w

a **ne**w bicycle

**Writing Tip** "**nu**" has two strokes: 1) a stop and 2) looping stop.

Trace these characters.

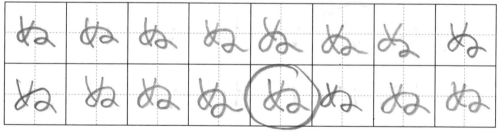

Write the character in the boxes below, and then circle the one you think is best.

1. **i nu** (dog)

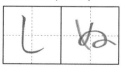

2. **nu i gu ru mi** (stuffed animal)

3. **shi nu** (to die)

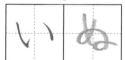

4. **nu ru** (to paint; to color)

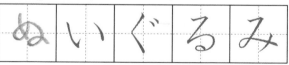

5. **nu ma** (swamp; pond)

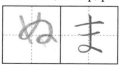

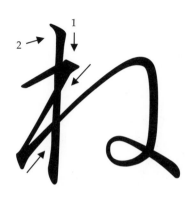

"**ne**" as in **ne**st

a **ne**st in a tree

**Writing Tip** "ne" has two strokes: 1) a stop and 2) zigzag, looping stop. (It looks like a "1," "7" and "2" all together).

Trace these characters.

Write the character in the boxes below, and then circle the one you think is best.

1. **ne ko** (cat)

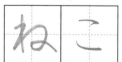

2. **mu ne** (chest)

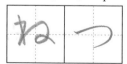

3. **o ka ne** (money)

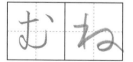

4. **ne ru** (to sleep; lie down)

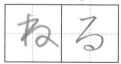

5. **ne tsu** (fever; temperature)

6. **fu ne** (boat)

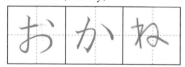

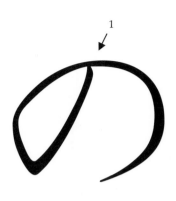

"**no**" as in <u>**no**</u>

<u>**No**</u> parking!

**Writing Tip** "no" has one stroke: a circling brush.

Trace these characters.

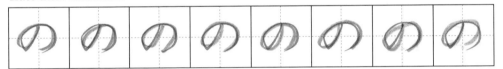

Write the character in the boxes below, and then circle the one you think is best.

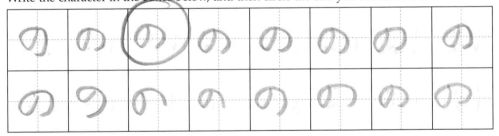

1. **no ri** (glue)

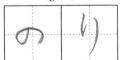

2. **no do** (throat)

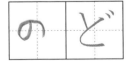

3. **mo no** (thing; object)

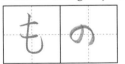

4. **no mi mo no** (beverage; drink)

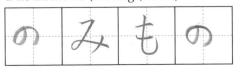

5. **ki nō** (yesterday)

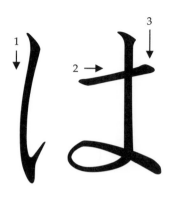

"**ha**" as in **ha**ll

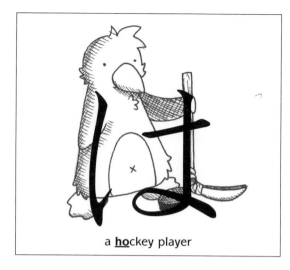

a **ho**ckey player

**Writing Tip** "**ha**" has three strokes: 1) a jump, 2) stop and 3) looping stop.

Trace these characters.

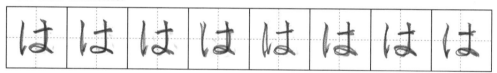

Write the character in the boxes below, and then circle the one you think is best.

1. **ha ru** (spring)

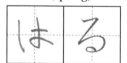

2. **ha i** (Yes!)

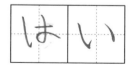

3. **ha ko** (box)

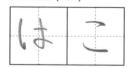

4. **ha sa mi** (scissors)

5. **ha** (tooth; teeth)

6. **ha re** (fine weather)

1 →

"**hi**" as in <u>he</u>.

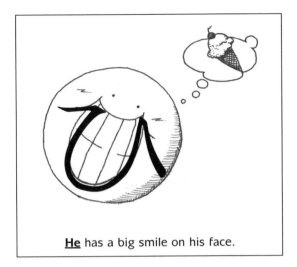

<u>He</u> has a big smile on his face.

**Writing Tip** "hi" has one stroke: a sweeping stop.

Trace these characters.

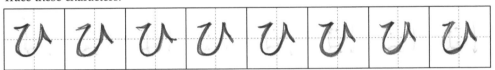

Write the character in the boxes below, and then circle the one you think is best.

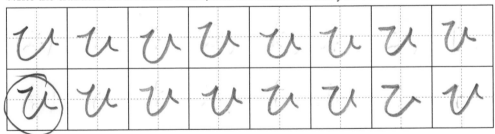

1. **hi to** (person)

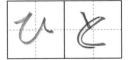

2. **hi za** (knee; lap)

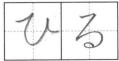

3. **hi ji** (elbow)

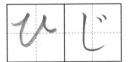

4. **hi** (fire; flame) 5. **hi ru** (noon; daytime)　6. **hi tsu ji** (sheep)

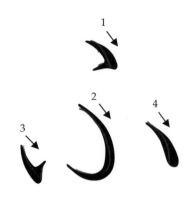

"fu" as in <u>who</u>
(except the lips are less rounded and more air escapes from the mouth)

Mount <u>Fu</u>ji is a dormant volcano. (Pronounce "fu" without touching the upper teeth and lower lip.)

**Writing Tip** "fu" has four strokes: 1) a jump, 2) brush, 3) jump and 4) stop.

Trace these characters.

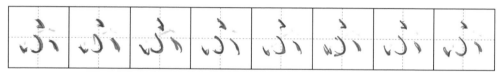

Write the character in the boxes below, and then circle the one you think is best.

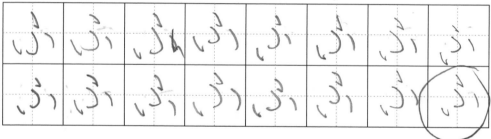

1. **fu ji** (Mount Fuji)

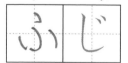

2. **fu yu** (winter)

3. **tō fu** (tofu)

4. **fu to n** (futon mattress)

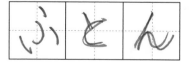

5. **o fu ro** (bathtub)

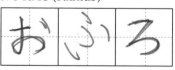

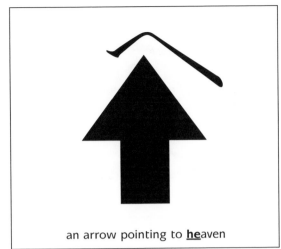

"**he**" as in **he**aven

an arrow pointing to **he**aven

**Writing Tip** "he" has one stroke: a stop.

Trace these characters.

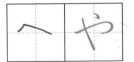

Write the character in the boxes below, and then circle the one you think is best.

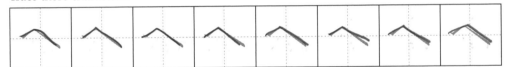

1. **he ya** (room; bedroom)  2. **he bi** (snake)

3. **he n** (odd; strange)

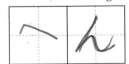

4. **he ta** (unskillful)  5. **o he so** (navel; belly button)

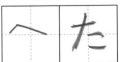

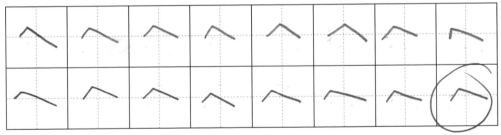

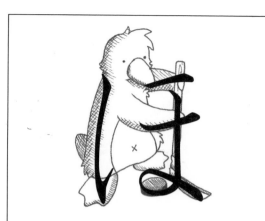

"**ho**" as in <u>ho</u>ld

<u>Ho</u>lding the hockey stick with two hands, he is ready to play!

**Writing Tip** "ho" has four strokes: 1) a jump, 2) stop, 3) stop and 4) looping stop.

Trace these characters.

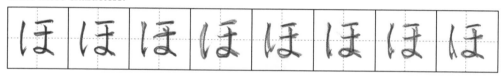

Write the character in the boxes below, and then circle the one you think is best.

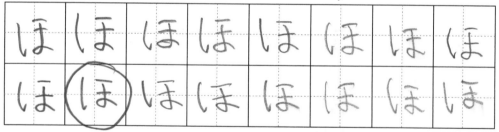

1. **ho n** (books)

2. **ho shi** (stars)

3. **ho ne** (bones)

4. **e ho n** (picture books)

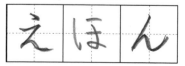

5. **ho so i** (thin; slender)

## READING PRACTICE 2: た～ほ

You should now be able to read the words below. Fold the page lengthwise (or cover it with your hand) so you can only see the hiragana words on the left hand side of the page. Try reading them aloud and then check with the words on the right. Keep practicing until you can read them all. For an extra challenge try reading the Japanese and saying the English word before checking.

| | | | | |
|---|---|---|---|---|
| い | た | い | | **i ta i** (Ouch!) |
| た | の | し | い | **ta no shi i** (fun) |
| し | た | た | | **shi ta** (under; below; tongue) |
| い | ち | ち | | **i chi** (one) |
| う | ち | ち | | **u chi** (home; house) |
| あ | つ | い | | **a tsu i** (hot) |
| く | つ | | | **ku tsu** (shoes) |
| ち | か | て | つ | **chi ka te tsu** (subway; underground train) |
| ひ | と | | | **hi to** (person) |
| そ | と | | | **so to** (outside) |
| な | つ | | | **na tsu** (summer) |
| く | に | | | **ku ni** (country; nation) |
| に | く | | | **ni ku** (meat) |
| い | ぬ | | | **i nu** (dog) |
| し | ぬ | | | **shi nu** (to die) |
| ね | こ | | | **ne ko** (cat) |
| お | か | ね | | **o ka ne** (money) |
| は | い | | | **ha i** (Yes!) |
| は | こ | | | **ha ko** (box) |
| ひ | き | に | く | **hi ki ni ku** (ground meat; minced meat) |
| ひ | | | | **hi** (fire; flame) |
| ふ | え | | | **fu e** (flute) |
| ふ | ゆ | | | **fu yu** (winter) |
| お | へ | そ | | **o he so** (navel; belly button) |
| へ | た | | | **he ta** (unskillful) |
| ほ | そ | い | | **ho so i** (thin; slender) |
| ほ | し | | | **ho shi** (stars) |

| | |
|---|---|
| Romaji pronunciation guide: | |
| *a* | as in **father** |
| *i* | as in **easy** |
| *u* | as in **you** |
| *e* | as in **red** |
| *o* | as in **oak** |

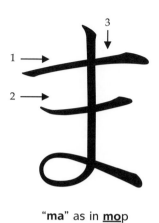

"**ma**" as in **mo**p

He will **mop** the floor.

**Writing Tip** "**ma**" has three strokes: 1) a stop, 2) stop and 3) a looping stop.

Trace these characters.

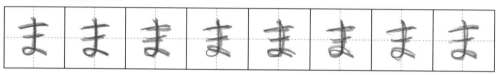

Write the character in the boxes below, and then circle the one you think is best.

1. **ma zu i** (unpleasant – taste or situation)

2. **a ma i** (sweet; indulgent)

3. **se ma i** (narrow; confining)

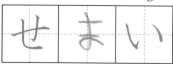

4. **i ma** (living room)

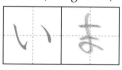

5. **ma do** (window)

"mi" as in <u>me</u>

Who is number 21? <u>Me</u>!

**Writing Tip** "mi" has two strokes: 1) a looping stop and 2) brush.

Trace these characters.

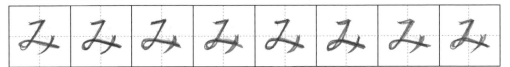

Write the character in the boxes below, and then circle the one you think is best.

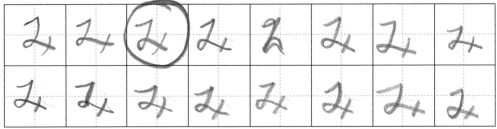

1. **mi mi** (ears)

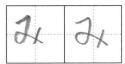

2. **mi gi** (right hand side)

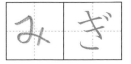

3. **mi zu** (water)

4. **ya su mi** (vacation; holiday)

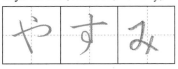

5. **sa shi mi** (sliced raw fish)

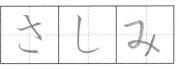

"**mu**" as in **moo**

**Moo**!

**Writing Tip** "**mu**" has three strokes: 1) a stop, 2) looping brush and 3) stop.

Trace these characters.

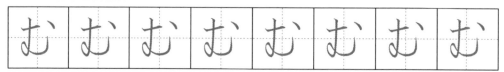

Write the character in the boxes below, and then circle the one you think is best.

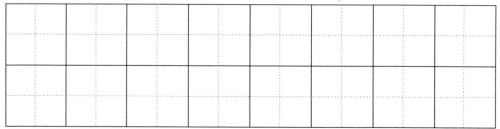

1. **mu ra sa ki** (purple)

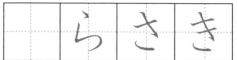

2. **sa mu ra i** (samurai warrior)

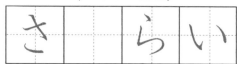

3. **ya su mu** (to rest; take a day off)

4. **no mu** (to drink)

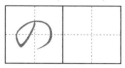

5. **su mu** (to live)

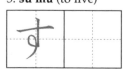

"**me**" as in <u>Me</u>xico

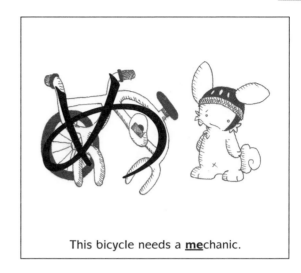

This bicycle needs a <u>me</u>chanic.

**Writing Tip** "**me**" has two strokes: 1) a stop and 2) looping brush.

Trace these characters.

Write the character in the boxes below, and then circle the one you think is best.

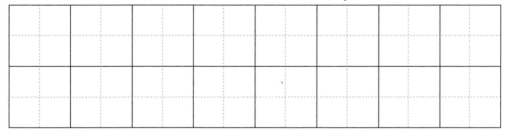

1. **me** (eyes)

2. **tsu me ta i** (cold to the touch)

3. **ka me** (turtle)

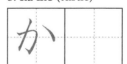

4. **tsu me** (fingernail)

5. **go me n na sa i** (I'm sorry.)

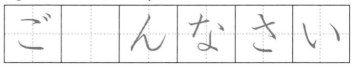

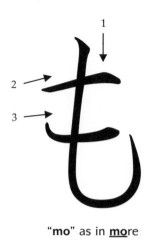

"**mo**" as in <u>mo</u>re

You can catch <u>mo</u>re fish with <u>mo</u>re bait.

**Writing Tip** "**mo**" has three strokes: 1) a brush, 2) stop and 3) stop.

Trace these characters.

Write the character in the boxes below, and then circle the one you think is best.

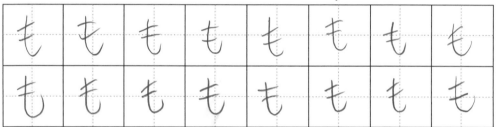

1. **mo mo** (peach)

2. **mo shi mo shi** (hello – on the phone)

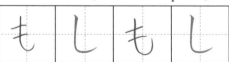

3. **i tsu mo** (always)

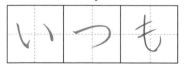

4. **to mo da chi** (friends)

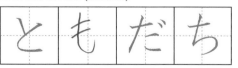

"**ya**" as in **ya**rn

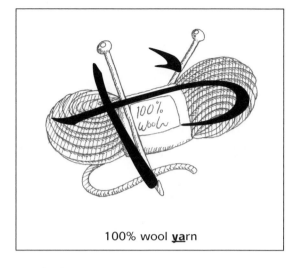

100% wool **ya**rn

**Writing Tip** "**ya**" has three strokes: 1) a brush, 2) jump and 3) stop.

Trace these characters.

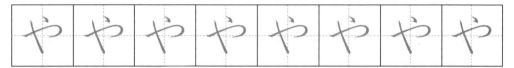

Write the character in the boxes below, and then circle the one you think is best.

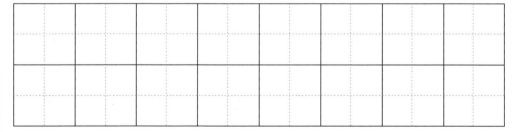

1. **ya sa i** (vegetables)

2. **ya su i** (inexpensive)

3. **ya o ya** (vegetable stand)

4. **ha ya i** (fast; early)

1

2

"**yu**" as in **you**

**You** stabbed the fish!

**Writing Tip** "yu" has two strokes and they are both brushes.

Trace these characters.

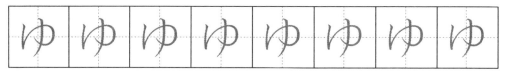

Write the character in the boxes below, and then circle the one you think is best.

**1. yu bi** (finger)

**2. yu ka** (floor)

**3. yu me** (dream)

**4. yū bi n** (mail; postal service)

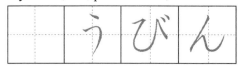

**5. yo yū** (spare – time, money, etc)

"**yo**" as in <u>yo-yo</u>

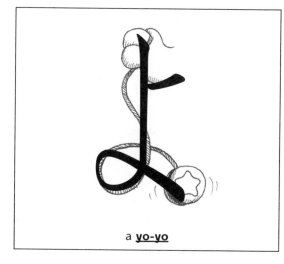

a <u>yo-yo</u>

**Writing Tip** "yo" has two strokes and both of them are stops.

Trace these characters.

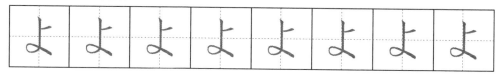

Write the character in the boxes below, and then circle the one you think is best.

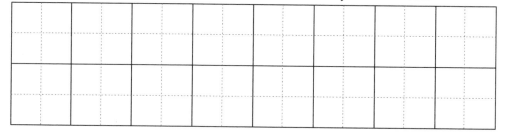

1. **yo ru** (evening; night)    2. **sa yō na ra** (goodbye)

3. **yo wa i** (weak)

4. **tsu yo i** (strong)

"ra" as in <u>Ra</u>h! <u>Ra</u>h! <u>Ra</u>h!

Using a megaphone the fan cheered for the team: <u>Ra</u>h! <u>Ra</u>h! <u>Ra</u>h!

**Writing Tip** "ra" has two strokes: 1) a jump and 2) brush.

Trace these characters.

Write the character in the boxes below, and then circle the one you think is best.

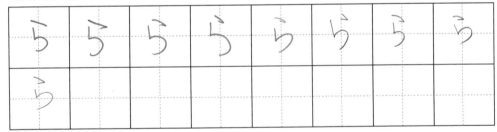

1. **o te a ra i** (restroom)

2. **i ku ra** (how much?)

3. **ka ra i** (spicy; hot)

4. **ki ra i** (dislike – adjective)

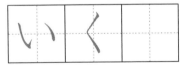

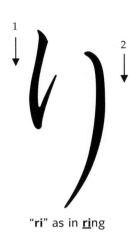

1 ↓    2 ↓

"**ri**" as in <u>ri</u>ng

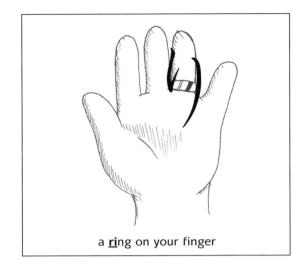

a <u>ri</u>ng on your finger

**Writing Tip** "**ri**" has two strokes: 1) a jump and 2) brush.

Trace these characters.

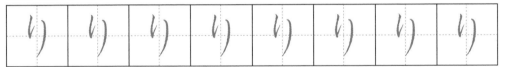

Write the character in the boxes below, and then circle the one you think is best.

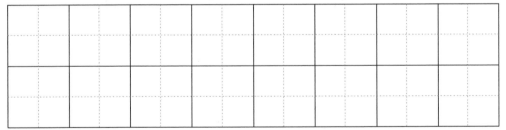

1. **i ri gu chi** (entrance)

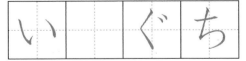

2. **ku su ri** (medicine)

3. **o tsu ri** (change – money)

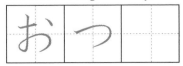

4. **ku mo ri** (cloudy)

"**ru**" as in <u>ru</u>by

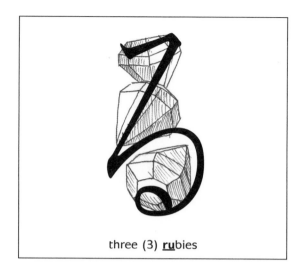

three (3) <u>ru</u>bies

**Writing Tip** "ru" has one stroke: a zigzag-looping stop.

Trace these characters.

Write the character in the boxes below, and then circle the one you think is best.

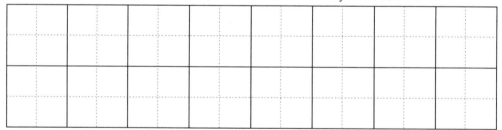

1. **fu ru i** (old - not person)

2. **a ru ku** (to walk)

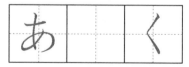

3. **ka e ru** (frog; to return home)

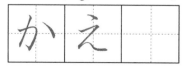

4. **zu ru i** (unfair; cunning)

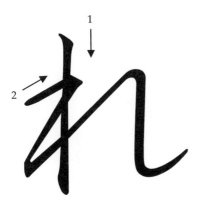

"**re**" as in **ra**dio

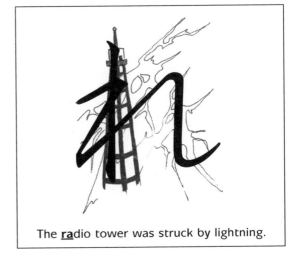

The **ra**dio tower was struck by lightning.

**Writing Tip** "**re**" has two strokes: 1) a stop and 2) zigzag brush.

Trace these characters.

Write the character in the boxes below, and then circle the one you think is best.

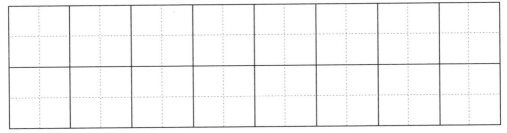

1. **da re** (who)

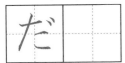

2. **ki re i** (pretty; clean; tidy)

3. **a re** (that over there)

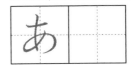

4. **u re shi i** (happy; glad)

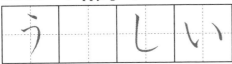

5. **i re ru** (to insert; to put in)

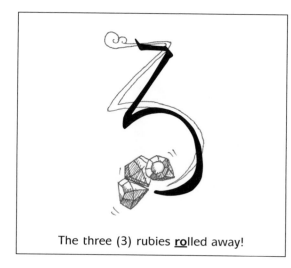

"**ro**" as in **ro**ll

The three (3) rubies **ro**lled away!

**Writing Tip** "ro" has one stroke: a zigzag brush.

Trace these characters.

Write the character in the boxes below, and then circle the one you think is best.

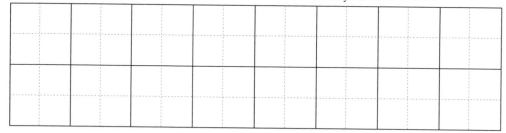

1. **te bu ku ro** (gloves)

2. **u shi ro** (behind)

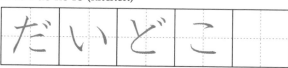

3. **hi ro i** (wide; spacious)

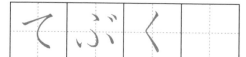

4. **da i do ko ro** (kitchen)

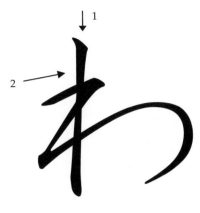

"**wa**" as in **wa**ter

A **wa**terfall is rushing past a tree.

**Writing Tip** "wa" has two strokes: 1) a stop and 2) zigzag brush.

Trace these characters.

Write the character in the boxes below, and then circle the one you think is best.

1. **wa ta shi** (I; myself)

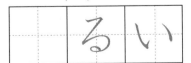

2. **de n wa** (telephone)

3. **wa ru i** (bad)

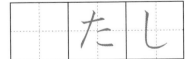

4. **su wa ru** (to sit)

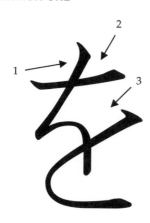

"**o**" as in <u>o</u>ld
(same pronunciation as お)

"Wh<u>oa</u>!" calls the cowboy to his horse.
(the "**w**" is dropped in modern Japanese)

**Writing Tip** "o" has three strokes and they are all stops.

Trace these characters.

Write the character in the boxes below, and then circle the one you think is best.

This character is not used to write words; it is a grammatical object marker (see Section Two).
Trace the light gray characters and write the character "o" by yourself.

1. **watashi wa sono hon o yomimasu** (I will read that book.)

わたし は そのほん ☐ よみます。

2. **dare ga momo o tabemashita ka** (Who ate the peach?)

だれ が もも ☐ たべましたか。

"n"as in **in**k
(pronounced by touching the back of the tongue to the roof of the mouth)

The single consonant syllable "**n**" looks and sounds a little like the English letter "**n**."

**Writing Tip** "n" has one stroke: a brush.

Trace these characters.

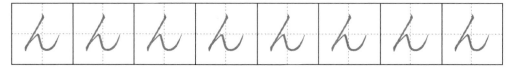

Write the character in the boxes below, and then circle the one you think is best.

1. **su mi ma se n** (Excuse me.)

2. **e n** (Yen – money)

3. **ta n su** (chest of drawers)

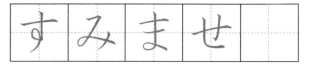

4. **shi n shi tsu** (bedroom)

## READING PRACTICE 3: ま ～ ん

You should now be able to read the words below. Fold the page lengthwise (or cover it with your hand) so you can only see the hiragana words on the left hand side of the page. Try reading them aloud and then check with the words on the right. Keep practicing until you can read them all. For an extra challenge try reading the Japanese and saying the English word before checking.

|  | | | | |  |
|---|---|---|---|---|---|
| あ | ま | い | | | **a ma i** (sweet; indulgent) |
| い | ま | | | | **i ma** (living room) |
| や | す | み | | | **ya su mi** (vacation; holiday) |
| み | み | | | | **mi mi** (ears) |
| む | ら | さ | き | | **mu ra sa ki** (purple) |
| さ | む | ら | い | | **sa mu ra i** (samurai warrior) |
| め | | | | | **me** (eyes) |
| か | め | | | | **ka me** (turtle) |
| も | し | も | し | | **mo shi mo shi** (hello – on the phone) |
| も | も | | | | **mo mo** (peach) |
| や | す | い | | | **ya su i** (inexpensive) |
| や | お | や | | | **ya o ya** (vegetable stand) |
| ゆ | か | | | | **yu ka** (floor) |
| ゆ | め | | | | **yu me** (dream) |
| さ | よ | う | な | ら | **sa yō na ra** (goodbye) |
| よ | る | | | | **yo ru** (evening; night) |
| い | く | ら | | | **i ku ra** (how much) |
| か | ら | い | | | **ka ra i** (spicy; hot) |
| お | つ | り | | | **o tsu ri** (change – money) |
| く | す | り | | | **ku su ri** (medicine) |
| ふ | る | い | | | **fu ru i** (old – not person) |
| か | え | る | | | **ka e ru** (frog; to return home) |
| き | れ | い | | | **ki re i** (pretty; clean; tidy) |
| う | れ | し | い | | **u re shi i** (happy; glad) |
| ひ | ろ | い | | | **hi ro i** (wide; spacious) |
| う | し | ろ | | | **u shi ro** (behind) |
| わ | た | し | | | **wa ta shi** (I; myself) |
| か | わ | い | い | | **ka wa i i** (cute) |
| え | ん | | | | **e n** (yen – Japanese money) |

Romaji pronunciation guide:

| | |
|---|---|
| *a* | as in **father** |
| *i* | as in **easy** |
| *u* | as in **you** |
| *e* | as in **red** |
| *o* | as in **oak** |

# SECTION TWO
# Hiragana Usage Rules

## THE ADDITIONAL 58 HIRAGANA SOUNDS

| | | | | |
|---|---|---|---|---|
| ga が | gi ぎ | gu ぐ | ge げ | go ご |
| za ざ | ji じ | zu ず | ze ぜ | zo ぞ |
| da だ | ji* ぢ | zu* づ | de で | do ど |
| ba ば | bi び | bu ぶ | be べ | bo ぼ |
| pa ぱ | pi ぴ | pu ぷ | pe ぺ | po ぽ |

\* "ji" and "zu" are usually written with じ and ず.

| | | |
|---|---|---|
| kya きゃ | kyu きゅ | kyo きょ |
| sha しゃ | shu しゅ | sho しょ |
| cha ちゃ | chu ちゅ | cho ちょ |
| nya にゃ | nyu にゅ | nyo にょ |
| hya ひゃ | hyu ひゅ | hyo ひょ |

| | | |
|---|---|---|
| gya ぎゃ | gyu ぎゅ | gyo ぎょ |
| ja じゃ | ju じゅ | jo じょ |
| ja* ぢゃ | ju* ぢゅ | jo* ぢょ |

\* "ja," "ju" and "jo" are usually written with じゃ, じゅ and じょ.

| | | |
|---|---|---|
| mya みゃ | myu みゅ | myo みょ |
| rya りゃ | ryu りゅ | ryo りょ |

| | | |
|---|---|---|
| bya びゃ | byu びゅ | byo びょ |
| pya ぴゃ | pyu ぴゅ | pyo ぴょ |

Japanese learners are lucky that there are so few hiragana rules. Mastering all the rules (and exceptions) in English takes years of spelling tests. In Japanese, however, once you have learned the five basic rules of hiragana you will be able to write 58 additional sounds using the 46 hiragana characters already introduced, and write any word you like.

## RULE 1   TENTEN ( ˋ ) AND MARU ( ° )

The first rule describes the way the pronunciation changes when two small dashes ( ˋ ) called **tenten** or a small circle ( ° ) called **maru** is added to a hiragana character. Tenten may be added to 20 hiragana characters, giving them a voiced consonant sound. For example, adding tenten to any of the か, き, く, け, こ row characters changes the "k" (as in coat) to "g" (as in **goat**). You will notice a vibration in your throat when you pronounce "g," but not "k." All 20 hiragana characters become voiced sounds when you add tenten.

k˙ → g as in "goat"   t˙ → d as in "dye"   Except じ = ji (as in "jeans")
s˙ → z as in "zoo"   h˙ → b as in "big"   ぢ = ji (as in "jeans")
づ = zu (as in "zoo")

You may have noticed that there are two ways to write the sounds "ji" and "zu." In most cases "ji" and "zu" are written じ and ず.

Maru ( ° ) are only added to the hiragana characters は, ひ, ふ, へ, ほ. They become ぱ, ぴ, ぷ, ぺ, ぽ and they are pronounced "pa," "pi," "pu," "pe," "po."

h° → p as in "pig"

**Writing Practice:** Say the sounds aloud as you write these hiragana characters with tenten and maru. Trace the light gray characters and then complete the row by yourself.

| | | | | | | | |
|---|---|---|---|---|---|---|---|
| が ga | が | が | | | | | |
| ぎ gi | ぎ | ぎ | | | | | |
| ぐ gu | ぐ | ぐ | | | | | |
| げ ge | げ | げ | | | | | |

Now try writing the following words that use the first group of characters written with tenten.
Trace the light gray characters, and then write the appropriate character in the blank box.

**1. hi ra ga na** (hiragana)

**2. ma n ga** (comics)

**3. o ni gi ri** (rice ball)

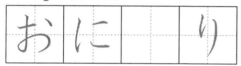

**4. mi gi** (right hand side)

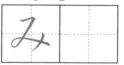

**5. i ri gu chi** (entrance)

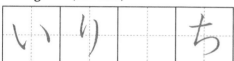

**6. o yo gu** (to swim)

**7. ge n ka n** (entryway of a Japanese home)

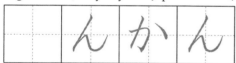

**8. ge n ki** (fine, healthy)

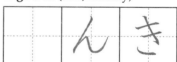

**9. ni ho n go** (Japanese language)

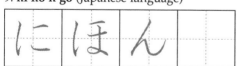

**10. go ha n** (rice; food)

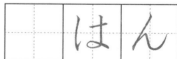

**11. me ga ne** (glasses)

**12. u sa gi** (rabbit)

13. **hi ge** (mustache, beard)  14. **de gu chi** (exit)

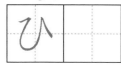 

The second group of characters written with tenten has one exception: じ is pronounced "**ji**."

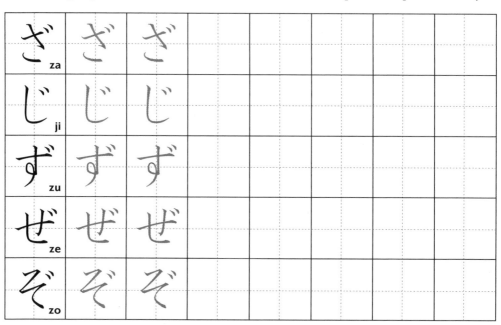

Try writing these words that use the second group of tenten characters.

1. **za n ne n** (unfortunate; too bad)

2. **hi za** (knee; lap)

3. **ji ka n** (time)

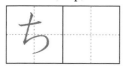

4. **hi tsu ji** (sheep)

5. **chi zu** (map)

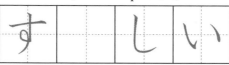

6. **su zu shi i** (cool – temperature)

7. **ka ze** (cold – illness; wind)     8. **ze n ze n** (not...at all; never)

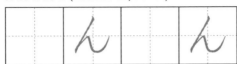

9. **zō** (elephant)     10. **ka zo ku** (family)

The third group of characters written with tenten has two exceptions: "**ji**" and "**zu**." As mentioned, there are two ways to write the sounds "**ji**" and "**zu**," but in most cases they are written with じ and ず. However, ぢ and づ are used in occasional compound words such as "bloody nose" (**ha na ji**) はなぢ and "hammer" (**ka na zu chi**) かなづち.

| | | | | | | | | |
|---|---|---|---|---|---|---|---|---|
| だ<br>**da** | だ | だ | | | | | | |
| ぢ<br>**ji** | ぢ | ぢ | | | | | | |
| づ<br>**zu** | づ | づ | | | | | | |
| で<br>**de** | で | で | | | | | | |
| ど<br>**do** | ど | ど | | | | | | |

Trace the light gray characters and then complete the word with the correct tenten character.

1. **to mo da chi** (friend)     2. **da re** (who)

3. **de n wa** (telephone)

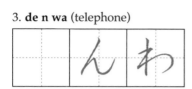

4. **de n ki** (light; electricity)

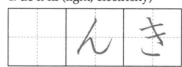

5. **da i do ko ro** (kitchen)

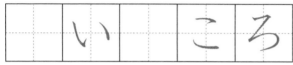

6. **ma do** (window)

The fourth group of characters written with tenten has no exceptions.

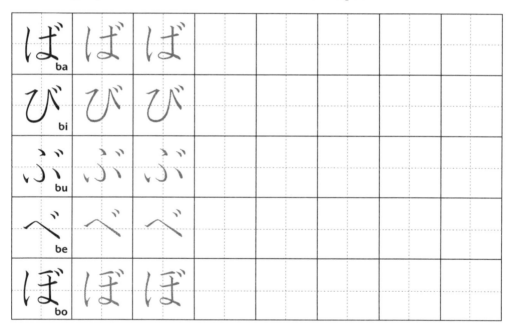

Try writing these words that use the fourth group of tenten characters.

1. **so ba** (buckwheat noodles)

2. **i ke ba na** (Japanese flower arranging)

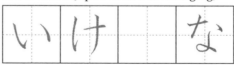

3. **ku bi** (neck)

4. **he bi** (snake)

5. **yu bi** (finger)

6. **shi n bu n** (newspaper)

7. **bu ta** (pig)

8. **su be te** (everything)

9. **ta be mo no** (food)

10. **bo ku** (I; me – used by boys)

11. **bo n sa i** (bonsai tree)

The small circle or maru ( ° ) is only added to "**ha**," "**hi**," "**fu**," "**he**" and "**ho**." Trace the light gray characters, and then try writing them in the blank boxes on your own.

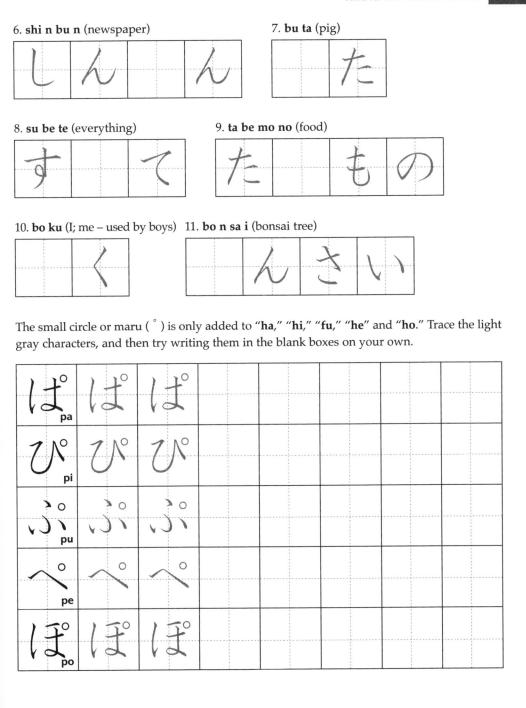

Try writing these words using characters written with maru ( ° ). Many of these words also use a small **"tsu"** (っ), which is pronounced as a short silent pause. In romaji a small **"tsu"** (っ) is usually indicated by doubling the following consonant (see Rule 3).

1. **su ppa i** (sour)

2. **ra ppa** (trumpet)

3. **e n pi tsu** (pencil)

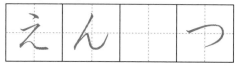

4. **ha ppi** (festival coat)

5. **te n pu ra** (battered, deep-fried food)

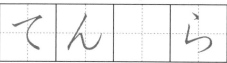

6. **ki ppu** (ticket)

7. **pe ra pe ra** (fluent; fluently)

8. **shi ppo** (tail of an animal)

9. **pe ko pe ko** (very hungry)

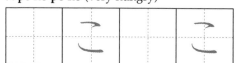

10. **po ka po ka** (warm feeling)

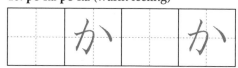

11. **ri ppa** (splendid; fine)

12. **ha ppa** (leaf)

## READING PRACTICE 4: TENTEN AND MARU

You should be able to read the words below now. Fold the page lengthwise (or cover it with your hand) so you can only see the hiragana words on the left half of the page. Try reading them aloud and then check your reading with the romaji on the right half of the page. Keep practicing until you can read them all.

| | | | | |
|---|---|---|---|---|
| ひ | ら | が | な | **hi ra ga na** (hiragana characters) |
| み | ぎ | | | **mi gi** (right hand side) |
| い | り | ぐ | ち | **i ri gu chi** (entrance) |
| げ | ん | か | ん | **ge n ka n** (entryway of a Japanese home) |
| に | ほ | ん | ご | **ni ho n go** (Japanese) |
| ひ | ざ | | | **hi za** (knee; lap) |
| じ | か | ん | | **ji ka n** (time) |
| ち | ず | | | **chi zu** (map) |
| か | ぜ | | | **ka ze** (cold – illness; wind) |
| か | ぞ | く | | **ka zo ku** (family) |
| だ | れ | | | **da re** (who) |
| で | ん | わ | | **de n wa** (telephone) |
| ま | ど | | | **ma do** (window) |
| い | け | ば | な | **i ke ba na** (flower arranging) |
| へ | び | | | **he bi** (snake) |
| し | ん | ぶ | ん | **shi n bu n** (newspaper) |
| す | べ | て | | **su be te** (all; everything) |
| ぼ | ん | さ | い | **bo n sa i** (bonsai tree) |
| ら | っ | ぱ | | **ra ppa** (trumpet) |
| え | ん | ぴ | つ | **e n pi tsu** (pencil) |
| き | っ | ぷ | | **ki ppu** (ticket) |
| ぺ | ら | ぺ | ら | **pe ra pe ra** (fluent; fluently) |
| し | っ | ぽ | | **shi ppo** (tail of an animal) |

## RULE 2   COMBINED CHARACTERS

As mentioned in the Introduction there are three special hiragana characters that are used extensively in combination with 11 consonants to form 33 additional sounds (see the chart at the beginning of Section Two). When combined in this way "**ya**," "**yu**" and "**yo**" are written in half-size characters at the bottom left corner, as in the examples below. Many of the example words have a line above the vowel, indicating it is two syllables in length. More information about Japanese long vowels will be explained later (see Rule 4). Trace the light gray characters and then try to complete the example words with the correct combined characters.

**kya**

き や

**kyu**

き ゅ

**kyo**

き ょ

1. **kya ku** (guest; customer)

く

2. **ya kyū** (baseball)

や う

3. **kyō** (today)

う

4. **kyū ri** (cucumber)

う り

**gya**

ぎ や

**gyu**

ぎ ゅ

**gyo**

ぎ ょ

1. **gya ku** (reverse; opposite)

く

2. **ki n gyo** (goldfish)

き ん

3. **gyū ni ku** (beef)

う に く

**sha**

し や

**shu**

し ゅ

**sho**

し ょ

1. **i sha** (medical doctor)

い

2. **shu fu** (homemaker)

ふ

3. **sho ku dō** (dining room; cafeteria)

く　ど　う

4. **ba sho** (place; location)

ば

**ja**

じゃ

**ju**

じゅ

**jo**

じょ

1. **jā ne** (See you later!)

あ　ね

2. **jū** (ten)

う

3. **ma jo** (witch)

ま

4. **jū sho** (address)

う　し　ょ

5. **ja ma** (nuisance)

ま

6. **jū dō** (judo)

う　ど　う

**cha**

ちゃ

**chu**

ちゅ

**cho**

ちょ

1. **o mo cha** (toys)

| お | も |  |  |

2. **cho tto** (a little; somewhat)

|  |  |  | っ | と |

3. **chū go ku** (China)

|  | う | ご | く |

4. **o cha** (green tea)

| お |  |  |

**ja**

| ぢ | ゃ |

**ju**

| ぢ | ゅ |

**jo**

| ぢ | ょ |

The above combined characters are rarely used, and they are usually used for emphasis only.

**nya**

| に | ゃ |

**nyu**

| に | ゅ |

**nyo**

| に | ょ |

1. **gyū nyū** (milk)

| ぎ | ゅ | う |  |  | う |

2. **nyā** (meow – cry of a cat)

|  |  | あ |

3. **ka nyū** (to subscribe)

| か |  |  | う |

4. **nyo ro nyo ro** (slithering(ly))

|  |  | ろ |  |  | ろ |

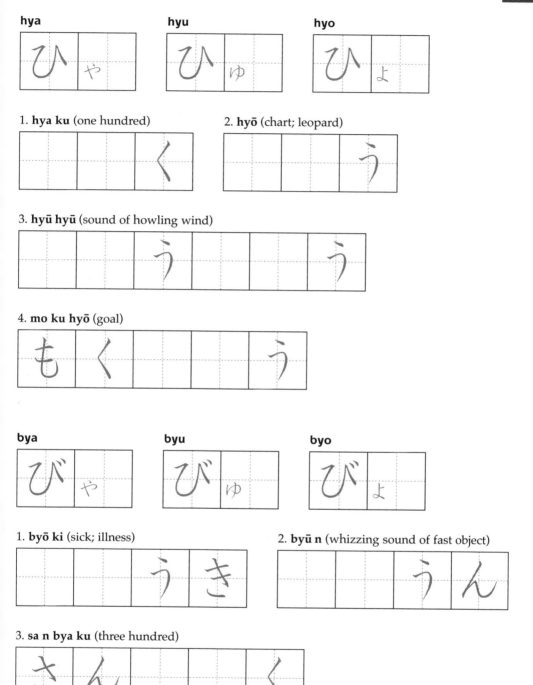

**hya**

ひ　や

**hyu**

ひ　ゆ

**hyo**

ひ　よ

1. **hya ku** (one hundred)

〈

2. **hyō** (chart; leopard)

う

3. **hyū hyū** (sound of howling wind)

う　　う

4. **mo ku hyō** (goal)

も　く　　　う

**bya**

び　や

**byu**

び　ゆ

**byo**

び　よ

1. **byō ki** (sick; illness)

う　き

2. **byū n** (whizzing sound of fast object)

う　ん

3. **sa n bya ku** (three hundred)

さ　ん　　　〈

**pya**

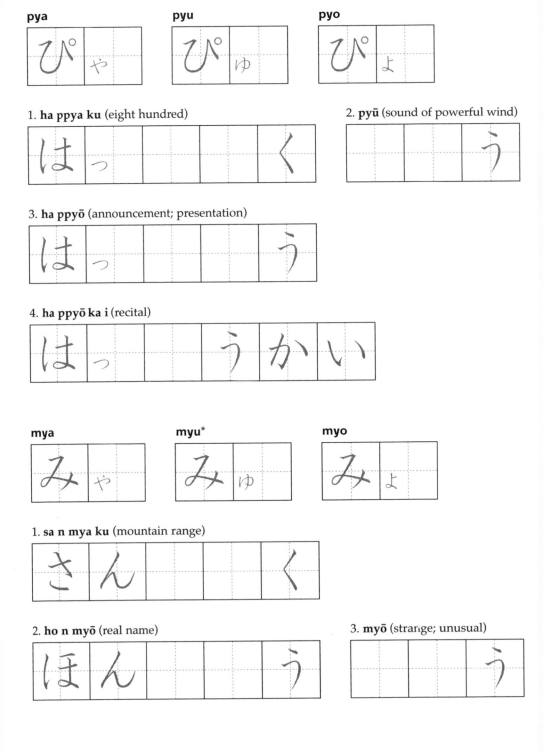

**pyu**

**pyo**

1. **ha ppya ku** (eight hundred)

2. **pyū** (sound of powerful wind)

3. **ha ppyō** (announcement; presentation)

4. **ha ppyō ka i** (recital)

**mya**

**myu***

**myo**

1. **sa n mya ku** (mountain range)

2. **ho n myō** (real name)

3. **myō** (strange; unusual)

*The character combination "myu" is only used in uncommon words not included here.

5. **mya ku** (pulse)

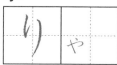

**rya**

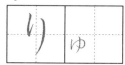

**ryu**

**ryo**

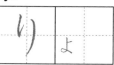

1. **rya ku go** (abbreviation)

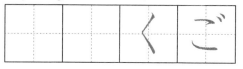

2. **ryo kō** (travel)

3. **ryū ga ku** (study abroad)

4. **ryō** (dormitory)

## READING PRACTICE 5: COMBINED CHARACTERS

You should be able to read these words with combined characters now. Fold the page lengthwise (or cover it with your hand) so you can only see the words on the left hand side of the page. Try reading them aloud and then check the words on the right. Keep practicing until you can read them all.

| | | | | | | |
|---|---|---|---|---|---|---|
| き | ゃ | く | | | | **kya ku** (guest; customer) |
| き | ゅ | う | り | | | **kyū ri** (cucumber) |
| き | ょ | う | と | | | **kyō to** (Kyoto) |
| き | ん | ぎ | に | く | | **ki n gyo** (goldfish) |
| き | ゅ | う | ゃ | | | **gyū ni ku** (beef) |
| ぎ | ゃ | く | ふ | | | **gya ku** (opposite; backwards) |
| い | し | ゃ | く | ど | う | **i sha** (doctor) |
| し | ゅ | ふ | ょ | | | **shu fu** (homemaker) |
| し | ょ | く | ん | ん | | **sho ku dō** (dining room; cafeteria) |
| ま | じ | ん | う | け | ぽ ん | **ma jo** (witch) |
| じ | ゃ | う | ち | し | ょ | **jan ken pon** (rock; paper; scissors) |
| じ | ゅ | ち | ゃ | | | **jū sho** (address) |
| お | も | | | | | **o mo cha** (toys) |

| | | | | | | |
|---|---|---|---|---|---|---|
| ち | ゅ | う | ご | く | | **chū go ku** (China) |
| ち | ょ | う | | | | **chō** (butterfly) |
| ぎ | ゅ | う | に | ゅ | う | **gyū nyū** (cows' milk) |
| ひ | ゃ | く | | | | **hya ku** (hundred) |
| ひ | ょ | う | | | | **hyō** (chart; leopard) |
| び | ょ | う | き | | | **byō ki** (sick; sickness) |
| さ | ん | び | ゃ | く | | **sa n bya ku** (three hundred) |
| み | ょ | う | | | | **myō** (strange; unusual) |
| り | ょ | う | | | | **ryō** (dormitory) |
| り | ゅ | う | が | く | | **ryū ga ku** (study abroad) |

## RULE 3   SMALL "TSU" (っ)

A small "**tsu**" (っ) is pronounced as a short silent pause. In romaji it is usually indicated by a doubling of the following consonant. One exception is the consonant "**ch**," in which case it is indicated by adding a "**t**" as in "**dotchi**" どっち or "which one; which way." A small "**tsu**" may also be used at the end of a phrase or sentence to indicate a sense of abruptness, anger, or surprise. It is pronounced with a "glottal stop" or in other words, stopping the flow of air by closing the back of the throat (epiglottis). Small "**tsu**" is written in the bottom left hand corner, as are small "**ya**," "**yu**," and "**yo**." Complete the example words by tracing the light gray characters and writing a small "**tsu**" in the appropriate area of the blank boxes.

Example of
regular-sized "**tsu**"

Example of
small "**tsu**"

1. **ga kkō** (school)

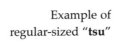

2. **a sa tte** (day after tomorrow)

3. **ki ssa te n** (coffee shop)

4. **ki tte** (stamp)

5. **ki ppu** (ticket)

6. **ma ssu gu** (straight)

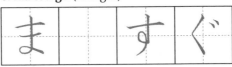

## READING PRACTICE 6: SMALL "tsu"

You should be able to read the words below with small "**tsu**" now. Remember to pronounce it as a short silent pause. Check your pronunciation with the phonetic guide on the right. If you don't understand, try reading Rule 3 again.

| Hiragana | Romaji |
|---|---|
| や っ た ！ | **ya tta**! (Yeah!) |
| た っ て く だ さ い | **ta tte ku da sa i** (Please stand!) |
| み っ つ | **mi ttsu** (three things) |
| よ っ つ | **yo ttsu** (four things) |
| む っ つ | **mu ttsu** (six things) |
| や っ つ | **ya ttsu** (eight things) |
| い っ さ い | **i ssa i** (one year old) |
| は っ さ い | **ha ssa i** (eight years old) |
| き っ て | **ki tte** (stamp) |
| か っ た | **ka tta** (I won.) |
| お も し ろ か っ た | **o mo shi ro ka tta** (That was fun.) |
| い ら っ しゃ い ま せ | **i ra ssha i ma se** (Welcome! – at stores) |
| ま っ す ぐ | **ma ssu gu** (straight) |
| い っ て く だ さ い | **i tte ku da sa i** (Please say it.) |
| に っ ぽ ん | **ni ppo n** (Japan – alternative name) |

## RULE 4    LONG VOWELS

As you have already seen many times, some words in romaji have a line above a vowel, indicating it is a long vowel, or a vowel two syllables in length. Writing most long vowels in hiragana is simple; you add one of the five Japanese vowels あ, い, う, え, お. As already noted, in romaji a long vowel is indicated by a line above the vowel, except "**i**," which is written twice. Read the examples below.

| | Hiragana | Romaji | |
|---|---|---|---|
| Long "**a**" | お か あ さ ん | **o kā sa n** | (mother) |
| Long "**i**" | い い え | **i i e** | (no) |
| Long "**u**" | き ゅ う り | **kyū ri** | (cucumber) |
| Long "**e**"* | お ね え さ ん | **o nē sa n** | (older sister) |
| Long "**o**"* | お お き い | **ō ki i** | (big) |

* Actually, the last two examples are exceptions. Usually い ("**i**" as in **ea**sy) makes the long え ("**e**" as in r**e**d) sound. Take extra care to pronounce an い following a character with the え vowel sound as a long vowel え. At first this may be a bit confusing because in romaji it is usually written with an "I." In this case the romaji reflects the hiragana writing, not the pronunciation.

| | |
|---|---|
| え い ご | **e i go (ē go)** (English) |
| せ ん せ い | **se n se i (se n sē)** (teacher) |
| え い が | **e i ga (ē ga)** (movie) |
| と け い | **to ke i (to kē)** (clock) |

Likewise, a long vowel お ("**o**" as in **o**ld) is made by adding う ("**u**" as in y**ou**th). This book consistently uses a line above the "**o**" to indicate the long vowel in romaji.

| | |
|---|---|
| さ よ う な ら | **sa yō na ra** (goodbye) |
| あ り が と う | **a ri ga tō** (thank you) |
| も う い ち ど | **mō i chi do** (one more time) |

## READING PRACTICE 7: LONG VOWELS

You should be able to read the words below with long vowels now. Cover the right hand side of the page so you can only see the hiragana words. Check your pronunciation with the phonetic guide on the right. If you don't understand, try reading Rule 4 again.

**o i shi i** (delicious)
**o kā sa n** (mother)
**tō kyō** (Tokyo; capital of Japan)
**ō ki i** (big)
**kyū** (nine)
**ki i ro** (yellow)
**ki re i** (pretty)
**hi kō ki** (airplane)
**o ni i sa n** (big brother)
**o ha yō** (good morning)
**o nē sa n** (big sister)
**ho n shū** (Honshū – island of Japan)
**o tō sa n** (dad)
**i i e** (no)
**kyō** (today)
**chi i sa i** (small)
**o tō to** (little brother)
**yo ne n se i** (fourth grader; senior)

| | | | | |
|---|---|---|---|---|
| じ | ゅ | う | | | **jū** (ten) |
| と | け | い | | | **to ke i** (clock) |
| あ | り | が | と | う | **a ri ga tō** (Thank you.) |
| お | ば | あ | さ | ん | **o bā sa n** (grandmother) |
| ふ | う | せ | ん | | **fū se n** (balloon) |
| じ | ゃ | あ | ね | | **jā ne** (See you later!) |
| が | っ | こ | う | | **ga kkō** (school) |
| お | じ | い | さ | ん | **o ji i sa n** (grandfather) |

## RULE 5  SENTENCE PARTICLES "WA," "E" AND "O"

Japanese uses small grammatical words called "particles" to help the reader understand the relationships between words in a sentence. They are usually one or two hiragana characters in length, and among other things, they indicate the topic, subject, object, location and direction. Particles are always placed directly after the words they mark. Rule 5 simply describes how three hiragana characters are pronounced differently when used as grammatical particles.

"**wa**" The Topic Particle:
When used as a "topic" particle, は is pronounced "**wa**" instead of "**ha**."

**Examples**: Trace the light gray characters and then write the particle "**wa**" in the blank box. A period in Japanese is written with a small circle in the bottom left corner of its own box. After you have written each sentence, practice reading it and take care to pronounce the particles correctly.

A) I am a (college) student.

| **watashi** | **wa** | **gakusei** | **desu** |
|---|---|---|---|
| (I, me) | (topic) | (student) | (am, are) |

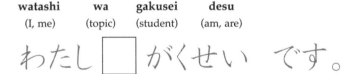

B) What is your telephone number?

| **o** | **denwa bangō** | **wa** | **nan** | **desu** | **ka** |
|---|---|---|---|---|---|
| (honorific) | (phone number) | (topic) | (what) | (is, are) | (question particle) |

"**e**" The Direction Particle:
When used as a "direction" particle, へ is pronounced like え ("**e**" as in r**e**d).

**Examples:**

A) We are going to Peace Park (Hiroshima).

| watashi-tachi | wa | heiwa-kō en | e | ikimasu |
|---|---|---|---|---|
| (we) | (topic) | (Peace Park) | (direction particle) | (will go) |

わたしたち は へいわこうえん ☐ いきます。

B) Please turn right.

| migi | e | magatte | kudasai |
|---|---|---|---|
| (right) | (direction) | (to turn) | (please) |

みぎ ☐ まがって ください。

 "**o**" The Object Particle:
The character を is only used as a particle to mark the "object" of a sentence and it is pronounced like お ("**o**" as in **o**ld).

**Examples:**

A) I saw Mount Fuji.

| watashi | wa | fuji san | o | mimashita |
|---|---|---|---|---|
| (I; me) | (topic) | (Mount Fuji) | (object) | (saw) |

わたし は ふじさん ☐ みました。

B) I ate sushi yesterday.

| kinō | watashi | wa | sushi | o | tabemashita |
|---|---|---|---|---|---|
| (yesterday) | (I; me) | (topic) | (sushi) | (object) | (ate) |

きのう わたし は すし ☐ たべました。

## READING PRACTICE 8: PARTICLES "wa," "e" AND "o"

You should be able to read some sentences with the particles "wa," "e" and "o" now. Without looking at the phonetic guides on the bottom of the page try reading these sentences. Check your pronunciation when you are done. You may want to repeat this practice to increase accuracy and fluency.

1. せんしゅう は ふゆやすみ でした。

2. わたし は ともだち の うち へ いきました。

3. えいが を みました。

4. ともだち は まいにち おかし を たべます。

5. らいしゅう はいしゃ へ いきます。

6. ともだち は はいしゃ が きらい です。

7. はる やすみ は いつ ですか。

8. どこ へ いきますか。

9. なに を しますか。

10. わたし は らいねん にほん へ りゅうがく します。

11. にほんご を べんきょう します。

| | | |
|---|---|---|
| 1. | **sen shū wa fuyu yasumi deshita.** | Last week was winter break. |
| 2. | **watashi wa tomodachi no uchi e ikimashita.** | I went to a friend's house. |
| 3. | **eiga o mimashita.** | (We) saw a movie. |
| 4. | **tomodachi wa mainichi okashi o tabemasu.** | My friend eats snacks everyday. |
| 5. | **raishū haisha e ikimasu.** | (My friend) is going to the dentist next week. |
| 6. | **tomodachi wa haisha ga kirai desu.** | My friend hates the dentist. |
| 7. | **haru yasumi wa itsu desu ka.** | When is spring vacation? |
| 8. | **doko e ikimasu ka.** | Where will you go? |
| 9. | **nani o shimasu ka.** | What will you do? |
| 10. | **watashi wa rainen nihon e ryūgaku shimasu.** | I will study abroad in Japan next year. |
| 11. | **nihongo o benkyō shimasu.** | (I) will study Japanese. |

# SECTION THREE
# Reading and Writing Practice

Commonly Mistaken Hiragana

Commonly Mistaken Combined Characters

Map of Japan

Family Members

Daily Expressions

Numbers

Parts of the Body

Weather

Places at School

In the Classroom

At the Department Store

Japanese Foods

Japanese Lunch Kiosk

Animals

なまえ ＿＿＿＿＿＿＿＿＿

# Commonly Mistaken Hiragana

**Part A:**
Circle the correct hiragana character.

| i | け こ り ⓘ き ま も |
|---|---|
| 1. ku | し く つ て ん へ え |
| 2. a | お ぬ ゆ わ あ め ね |
| 3. sa | よ き を ち せ け さ |
| 4. ta | た な さ は も こ い |
| 5. nu | あ め わ ぬ お な ま |
| 6. ne | れ ね わ あ お ゆ の |
| 7. wa | ね あ れ め ぬ わ つ |
| 8. ma | も き ま に こ た ほ |
| 9. su | む る ぬ す み ね ま |
| 10. ri | い り こ ら う そ え |
| 11. ra | う え む ら お や な |
| 12. ke | い に り ほ は せ け |
| 13. so | ろ と て こ え そ ん |
| 14. tsu | て う ら つ め わ ち |
| 15. ni | こ い り た に ほ は |
| 16. ha | ほ け は に な も ま |
| 17. ya | か な つ う や ら め |

**Part B:**
Circle the correct hiragana character.

| ko | ほ い に た ⓒ も り |
|---|---|
| 1. shi | し つ へ く ん て と |
| 2. o | や な ⓞ め あ ね ぬ |
| 3. ki | さ よ を ち ま も ⓚ |
| 4. na | た な き は ほ も よ |
| 5. me | ぬ お あ ゆ わ め ね |
| 6. re | ぬ そ わ ね れ あ つ |
| 7. ro | ろ そ る を よ と え |
| 8. ho | は ま き ほ さ こ た |
| 9. mu | す む み ま ね ぬ る |
| 10. ru | ろ そ と よ む す る |
| 11. u | ら え や う お む な |
| 12. se | は け に た は せ り |
| 13. chi | さ つ た ろ ち を そ |
| 14. te | そ く て し つ へ ん |
| 15. no | の て あ ぬ め つ う |
| 16. mo | ま き ⓜ ほ け は し |
| 17. e | ん き う ら れ ⓔ そ |

Time ＿＿＿：＿＿＿

Time ＿＿＿：＿＿＿

なまえ _____

# Commonly Mistaken Combined Characters

**Part A:**
Circle the correct combined character.

|  |  |  |  |  |
|---|---|---|---|---|
| **gyo** | きょ | じょ | （ぎょ） | びょ |
| 1. **shu** | しゃ | しゅ | じゅ | ちゅ |
| 2. **cho** | ちゃ | ぢゃ | しょ | ちょ |
| 3. **myu** | みゅ | みょ | みゃ | ちゅ |
| 4. **bya** | ぴゃ | ひゃ | びゃ | びょ |
| 5. **gyu** | ぎゃ | きゅ | きょ | ぎゅ |
| 6. **nya** | にゅ | にゃ | りゃ | にょ |
| 7. **rya** | りゃ | にょ | りゅ | りょ |
| 8. **pyu** | ぴゃ | ひゅ | ぴょ | ぴゅ |
| 9. **jo** | じゃ | しょ | じょ | じゅ |
| 10. **kya** | ぎゃ | きゅ | きょ | きゃ |
| 11. **hyo** | ひゅ | ひょ | ぴょ | びょ |
| 12. **pyo** | ひょ | ぴょ | びょ | ぴゅ |
| 13. **kyu** | きゃ | ぎゅ | きゅ | きょ |
| 14. **sho** | しゅ | じゅ | しょ | じょ |
| 15. **byo** | ひょ | びゅ | ぴょ | びょ |

**Part B:**
Circle the correct combined character.

|  |  |  |  |  |
|---|---|---|---|---|
| **kyo** | びょ | ぎょ | きゅ | （きょ） |
| 1. **ju** | しゅ | じゅ | じゃ | じょ |
| 2. **nyo** | にょ | にゅ | りゅ | ちゅ |
| 3. **nyu** | にゅ | にゃ | にょ | りゅ |
| 4. **hya** | ひゅ | みゅ | りゅ | ひゃ |
| 5. **myo** | みゃ | りょ | みょ | ちょ |
| 6. **byu** | びゅ | ぴゅ | ひゅ | きゅ |
| 7. **ryo** | りゃ | りょ | ぴょ | りゅ |
| 8. **hyu** | ぴゅ | ひゃ | びゅ | ひゅ |
| 9. **chu** | ちゃ | しゅ | ちゅ | しゃ |
| 10. **ja** | しゃ | じゃ | しゅ | じゅ |
| 11. **cha** | しゃ | ちゅ | ちゃ | ちょ |
| 12. **ryu** | りゅ | りゃ | ちゃ | りょ |
| 13. **gya** | ぎゃ | しゅ | しゃ | ぎゅ |
| 14. **sha** | しゅ | しゃ | じゃ | じゅ |
| 15. **pya** | ぴゅ | びゃ | ぴゃ | ひゃ |

Time _____:_____

Time _____:_____

なまえ ______________

# Map of Japan

**Major Islands of Japan**

1. Hokkaido (**ho kka i dō**)

2. Honshu (**ho n shū**)

3. Shikoku (**shi ko ku**)

4. Kyushu (**kyū shū**)

5. Okinawa (**o ki na wa**)

Japan (**ni ho n**)

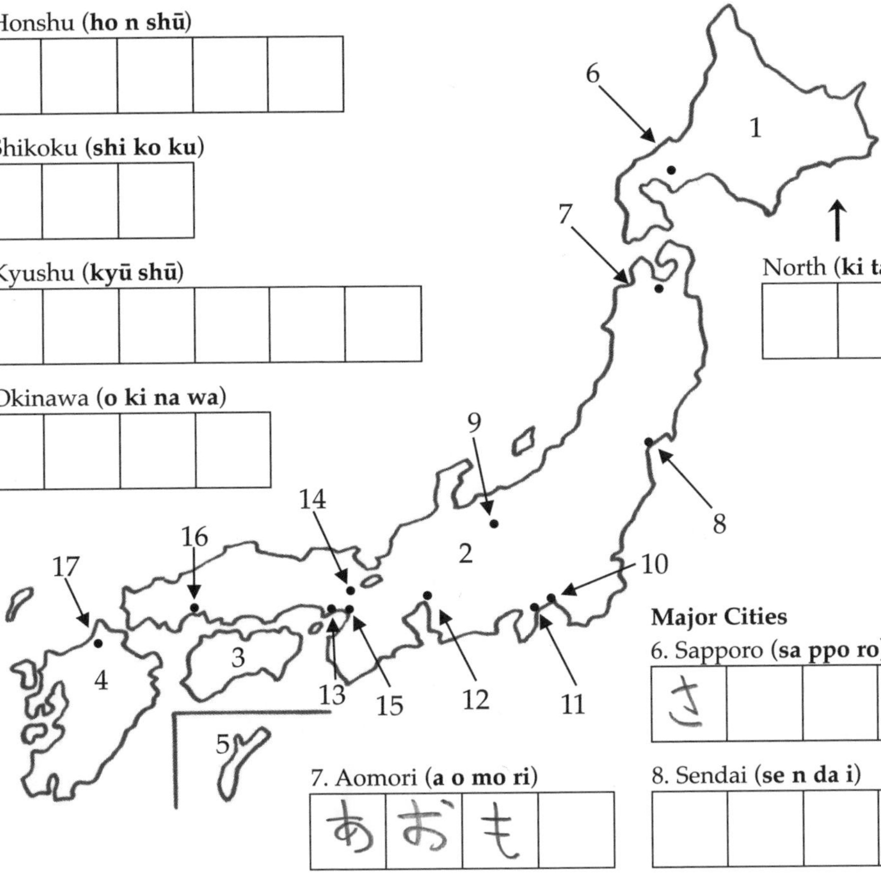


North (**ki ta**)

**Major Cities**

6. Sapporo (**sa ppo ro**)
さ

7. Aomori (**a o mo ri**)
あおも

8. Sendai (**se n da i**)

9. Nagano (**na ga no**)

10. Tokyo – capital (**tō kyō**)

11. Yokohama (**yo ko ha ma**)

12. Nagoya (**na go ya**)

13. Kobe (**kō be**)

14. Kyoto (**kyō to**)

15. Osaka (**ō sa ka**)

16. Hiroshima (**hi ro shi ma**)

17. Fukuoka (**fu ku o ka**)

なまえ ＿＿＿＿＿＿＿＿＿＿＿

# Family Members

| | | | | | | | | | | |
|---|---|---|---|---|---|---|---|---|---|---|
| と | も | わ | お | か | あ | さ | ん | お | え | お |
| お | う | た | か | ね | い | お | じ | さ | ん | と |
| に | と | し | へ | つ | し | ひ | す | た | あ | う |
| い | く | い | も | う | と | さ | て | ぼ | こ | さ |
| さ | せ | お | よ | み | お | ほ | ん | く | な | ん |
| ん | ち | ば | の | り | ば | ね | ら | か | め | お |
| あ | か | さ | ふ | を | あ | や | え | ゆ | ま | と |
| じ | ぬ | ん | む | れ | さ | い | と | さ | ん | う |
| し | お | じ | い | さ | ん | け | そ | き | ん | と |

1. I; myself – only boys (**bo ku**)

| | |
|---|---|
| | |

2. grandfather (**o ji i sa n**)

| お | | い | さ | ん |
|---|---|---|---|---|

3. I; myself (**wa ta shi**)

| | | |
|---|---|---|

4. grandmother (**o bā sa n**)

| お | | | | |
|---|---|---|---|---|

5. younger sister (**i mō to**)

| | | | |
|---|---|---|---|

6. father (**o tō sa n**)

| | | | |
|---|---|---|---|

7. younger brother (**o tō to**)

| | | | |
|---|---|---|---|

8. mother (**o kā sa n**)

| | | | |
|---|---|---|---|

9. uncle (**o ji sa n**)

| | | | |
|---|---|---|---|

10. older brother (**o ni i sa n**)

| | | | | |
|---|---|---|---|---|

11. aunt (**o ba sa n**)

| | | | |
|---|---|---|---|

12. older sister (**o nē sa n**)

| | | | |
|---|---|---|---|

## Daily Expressions

なまえ _____

namae

You're welcome! (**dō i ta shi mas hi te**)
Sounds like "Don't touch my mustache!"

**DOWN**

1. Excuse me. (**su mi ma se n**)
2. Hello!; Good afternoon! (**ko n ni chi wa***)
4. How are you? (**o ge n ki de su ka**)
5. Good night! (**o ya su mi na sa i**)
6. I'm sorry. (**go me n na sa i**)
10. You're welcome! (**dō i ta shi ma shi te**)
11. No. (**i i e**)

**ACROSS**

3. Good evening! (**ko n ba n wa***)
4. Good morning! (**o ha yō go za i ma su**)
7. I'm fine. (**ge n ki de su**)
8. Goodbye! (**sa yō na ra**)
9. Thank you. (**a ri ga tō go za i ma su**)
12. Yes. (**ha i**)

なまえ _____

## Numbers

Read the numbers in hiragana and connect them in the chart below. What do you see in the picture?

| | | | | |
|---|---|---|---|---|
| Start: きゅう(9)→ | じゅうはち(18)→ | にじゅうなな→ | さんじゅうなな→ | よんじゅうろく↓ |
| ↓ ななじゅうさん | ←ろくじゅうさん | ←ろくじゅうよん | ←ごじゅうご | ←ごじゅうろく |
| ななじゅうに→ | はちじゅういち→ | きゅうじゅういち→ | きゅうじゅうに→ | はちじゅうさん↓ |
| ↓きゅうじゅうよん | ←はちじゅうよん | ←ななじゅうご | ←ななじゅうよん | ←ななじゅうさん |
| はちじゅうご→ | ななじゅうご→ | ななじゅうろく→ | ろくじゅうなな→ | ごじゅうなな↓ |
| ↓ さんじゅう | ←さんじゅうきゅう | ←にじゅうはち | ←さんじゅうなな | ←よんじゅうなな |
| にじゅう→ | きゅう | Finished! | | |

| 1 | 2 | 3 | 4 | 5 | 6 | 7 | 8 | 9 | 10 |
|---|---|---|---|---|---|---|---|---|---|
| 11 | 12 | 13 | 14 | 15 | 16 | 17 | 18 | 19 | 20 |
| 21 | 22 | 23 | 24 | 25 | 26 | 27 | 28 | 29 | 30 |
| 31 | 32 | 33 | 34 | 35 | 36 | 37 | 38 | 39 | 40 |
| 41 | 42 | 43 | 44 | 45 | 46 | 47 | 48 | 49 | 50 |
| 51 | 52 | 53 | 54 | 55 | 56 | 57 | 58 | 59 | 60 |
| 61 | 62 | 63 | 64 | 65 | 66 | 67 | 68 | 69 | 70 |
| 71 | 72 | 73 | 74 | 75 | 76 | 77 | 78 | 79 | 80 |
| 81 | 82 | 83 | 84 | 85 | 86 | 87 | 88 | 89 | 90 |
| 91 | 92 | 93 | 94 | 95 | 96 | 97 | 98 | 99 | 100 |

(Hint: see page 87)

## Counting in Japanese

| | | | | | |
|---|---|---|---|---|---|
| 1 | いち | 11 | じゅういち | 30 | さんじゅう |
| 2 | に | 12 | じゅうに | 40 | よんじゅう；しじゅう |
| 3 | さん | 13 | じゅうさん | 50 | ごじゅう |
| 4 | よん；し | 14 | じゅうよん；じゅうし | 60 | ろくじゅう |
| 5 | ご | 15 | じゅうご | 70 | ななじゅう；しちじゅう |
| 6 | ろく | 16 | じゅうろく | 80 | はちじゅう |
| 7 | なな；しち | 17 | じゅうなな；じゅうしち | 90 | きゅうじゅう |
| 8 | はち | 18 | じゅうはち | 100 | ひゃく |
| 9 | きゅう；く | 19 | じゅうきゅう；じゅうく | | |
| 10 | じゅう | 20 | にじゅう | | |

なまえ _____

# Parts of the Body

1. head (**a ta ma**)

2. shoulders (**ka ta**)

3. knees (**hi za**)

4. legs; feet (**a shi**)

5. hands (**te**)

6. eyes (**me**)

7. ears (**mi mi**)

8. mouth (**ku chi**)

9. nose (**ha na**)

10. hair (**ka mi**)

11. stomach (**o na ka**)

12. back (**se na ka**)

13. face (**ka o**)

14. teeth (**ha**)

15. throat (**no do**)

16. neck (**ku bi**)

17. wrist (**te ku bi**)

18. ankle (**a shi ku bi**)

19. chest (**mu ne**)

20. arm (**u de**)

21. finger (**yu bi**)

22. fingernail (**tsu me**)

23. elbow (**hi ji**)

24. body (**ka ra da**)

# Common Expressions with Body Vocabulary

| | | |
|---|---|---|
| smart | あたま が いい | (literally "head is good") |
| dumb; unintelligent | あたま が わるい | (literally "head is bad") |
| poor hearing; deaf | みみ が とおい | (literally "ears are far") |
| bad eyesight | め が わるい | (literally "eyes are bad") |
| hungry | おなか が すいた | (literally "stomach became empty") |
| thirsty | のど が かわいた | (literally "throat became dry") |

なまえ _____

## Weather

1. weather (**te n ki**)

| | | |
|---|---|---|

2. clear; fine (**ha re**)

| | |
|---|---|

3. rain (**a me**)

| | |
|---|---|

4. cloudy (**ku mo ri**)

| | | |
|---|---|---|

5. snow (**yu ki**)

| | |
|---|---|

6. storm (**a ra shi**)

| | | |
|---|---|---|

7. windy (**ka ze ga tsu yo i**)

| | | | | | |
|---|---|---|---|---|---|

8. hot (**a tsu i**)

| | |
|---|---|

9. cold (**sa mu i**)

| | |
|---|---|

Describe today's weather as in the example below.

| Today's weather is <u>clear</u>. | きょう の てんき は <u>はれ</u> です。 |
|---|---|
| | Today  's  weather  "topic" particle  fine  is; am; are |

Try recording the weather for a month. Use hiragana to write the appropriate weather word(s) on the calendar below. Each time you record the weather, try describing it in Japanese.

| にち<br>Sunday | げつ<br>Monday | か<br>Tuesday | すい<br>Wednesday | もく<br>Thursday | きん<br>Friday | ど<br>Saturday |
|---|---|---|---|---|---|---|
| (date) | (date) | (date) | (date) | (date) | (date) | (date) |
| (date) | (date) | (date) | (date) | (date) | (date) | (date) |
| (date) | (date) | (date) | (date) | (date) | (date) | (date) |
| (date) | (date) | (date) | (date) | (date) | (date) | (date) |
| (date) | (date) | (date) | (date) | (date) | (date) | (date) |

なまえ _____

# Places at School

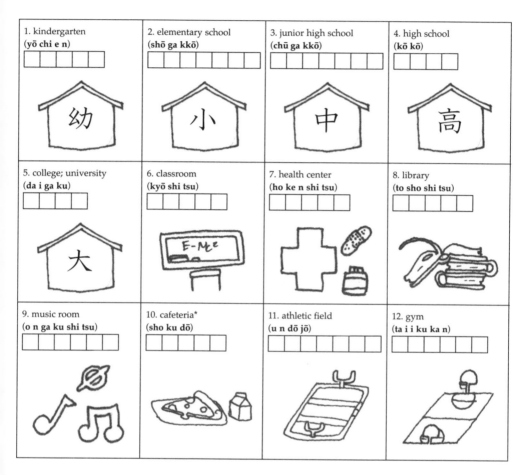

1. kindergarten
(yō chi e n)

2. elementary school
(shō ga kkō)

3. junior high school
(chū ga kkō)

4. high school
(kō kō)

幼　小　中　高

5. college; university
(da i ga ku)

6. classroom
(kyō shi tsu)

7. health center
(ho ke n shi tsu)

8. library
(to sho shi tsu)

大　E=Mc²

9. music room
(o n ga ku shi tsu)

10. cafeteria*
(sho ku dō)

11. athletic field
(u n dō jō)

12. gym
(ta i i ku ka n)

13. To which places do students usually bring books (please circle any that apply)?

きょうしつ　　　ほけんしつ　　　としょしつ　　　たいいくかん

14. Which schools come after Jr. High School (please circle any that apply)?

だいがく　　　しょうがっこう　　　こうこう　　　ようちえん

15. Which places are usually found indoors (please circle any that apply)?

としょしつ　　　ほけんしつ　　　うんどうじょう　　　おんがくしつ

*Japanese students (except university students) generally eat lunch in the classroom.

なまえ ＿＿＿＿＿＿＿＿＿＿

## In the Classroom

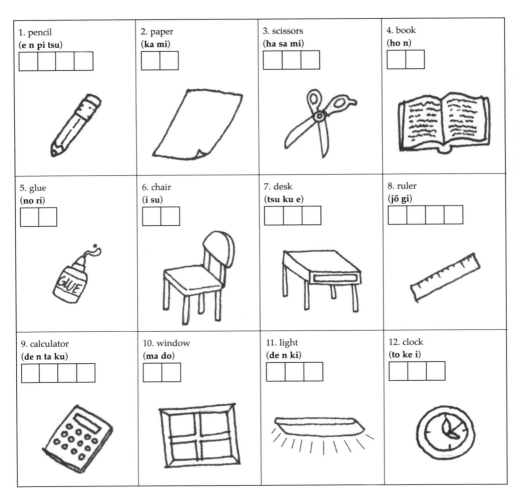

| 1. pencil (e n pi tsu) | 2. paper (ka mi) | 3. scissors (ha sa mi) | 4. book (ho n) |
|---|---|---|---|
| 5. glue (no ri) | 6. chair (i su) | 7. desk (tsu ku e) | 8. ruler (jō gi) |
| 9. calculator (de n ta ku) | 10. window (ma do) | 11. light (de n ki) | 12. clock (to ke i) |

13. Which objects could you fit into a backpack (circle any that apply)?

かみ　　　のり　　　いす　　　ほん　　　えんぴつ　つくえ

14. Which objects are too big to fit into a desk (circle any that apply)?

いす　　　はさみ　　まど　　　じょうぎ　　　のり　　　でんき

15. Which objects require electricity/batteries (circle any that apply)?

とけい　　　まど　　　でんたく　　　えんぴつ　　　でんき　　　のり

なまえ _____

# At the Department Store

Write in English and Japanese the appropriate floor of each item.

**Example:** clocks  <u>8th floor</u>

| は | ち | か | い |
|---|---|---|---|

1. kimono (**ki mo no**) _____

2. toys (**o mo cha**) _____

3. hats (**bō shi**) _____

4. books (**ho n**) _____

5. groceries (**sho ku hi n**) _____

6. rings (**yu bi wa**) _____

7. bags (**ka ba n**) _____

8. shoes (**ku tsu**) _____

9. suits (**se bi ro**) _____

10. gloves (**te bu ku ro**) _____

---

おもちゃ

10th floor (**ju kka i** or **ji kka i**)

ほん

9th floor (**kyū ka i**)

とけい

8th floor (**ha chi ka i**)

かばん

7th floor (**na na ka i**)

きもの

6th floor (**ro kka i**)

せびろ

5th floor (**go ka i**)

ぼうし

4th floor (**yo n ka i**)

てぶくろ

3th floor (**sa n ga i**)

くつ

2nd floor (**ni ka i**)

ゆびわ

1st floor (**i kka i**)

しょくひん

Basement 1st floor (**chi ka i kka i**)

なまえ _____

# Japanese Foods

| | | |
|---|---|---|
| 1. rice (**go ha n**) | 2. riceballs (**o ni gi ri**) | 3. box lunch (**o be n tō**) |
| 4. sushi (**su shi**) | 5. sliced raw fish (**sa shi mi**) | 6. thick white noodles (**u do n**) |
| 7. buckwheat noodles (**so ba**) | 8. chilled soba (**za ru so ba**) | 9. fried noodles (**ya ki so ba**) |
| 10. roasted chicken and vegetable kabob (**ya ki to ri**) | 11. battered and deep-fried seafood and vegetables (**te n pu ra**) | 12. roasted sweet potato (**ya ki i mo**) |

なまえ _____

# Japanese Lunch Kiosk
Read the menu and answer the questions below.

| | | | |
|---|---|---|---|
| おにぎり | 130 えん | やきいも | 300 えん |
| ごはん | 200 えん | やきとり | 400 えん |
| | | | |
| うどん | 350 えん | ぎゅうにゅう | 200 えん |
| そば | 350 えん | おちゃ | 200 えん |
| やきそば | 400 えん | こうちゃ | 200 えん |
| ざるそば | 350 えん | みず | 0 えん |
| | | | |
| すし　べんとう | 500 えん | | |
| てりやき　べんとう | 650 えん | | |
| てんぷら　べんとう | 750 えん | | |

Tell the price of the following lunch menu items.

**Example**: tempura box lunch (**te n pu ra be n tō**)? <u>750 えん</u>

1. How much is the sushi box lunch (**su shi be n tō**)? _____

2. How much is a rice ball (**o ni gi ri**)? _____

3. How much are the soba – buckwheat noodles (**so ba**)? _____

4. How much are the yakitori – roasted chicken and vegetables on a stick (**ya ki to ri**)?
_____

5. How much is rice (**go ha n**)? _____

6. What would you pay for green tea (**o cha**) and yakisoba – fried noodles (**ya ki so ba**)?
_____

7. What would you pay for water (**mi zu**) and a teriyaki box lunch (**te ri ya ki be n tō**)?
_____

8. What would you pay for milk (**gyū nyū**) and chilled soba noodles (**za ru so ba**)?
_____

なまえ _____

# Animals

Animals are generally found in one of three environments: 1. as a pet, 2. in the wild or zoo, or 3. on a farm. Write the name of each animal in hiragana in an appropriate category below.

| | | | |
|---|---|---|---|
| ☐ | Snake (**he bi**) | ☐ | Bear (**ku ma**) |
| ☐ | Dog (**i nu**) | ☐ | Pig (**bu ta**) |
| ☐ | Cow (**u shi**) | ☐ | Elephant (**zō**) |
| ☐ | Bird (**to ri**) | ☐ | Horse (**u ma**) |
| ☐ | Giraffe (**ki ri n**) | ☐ | Goldfish (**ki n gyo**) |
| ☐ | Rabbit (**u sa gi**) | ☐ | Cat (**ne ko**) |
| ☐ | Chicken (**ni wa to ri**) | ☐ | Fox (**ki tsu ne**) |
| ☐ | Monkey (**sa ru**) | ☐ | Alligator (**wa ni**) |
| ☐ | Turtle (**ka me**) | ☐ | Deer (**shi ka**) |
| ☐ | Tiger (**to ra**) | ☐ | Frog (**ka e ru**) |
| ☐ | Sheep (**hi tsu ji**) | ☐ | Squirrel (**ri su**) |

| Pets | Wild / Zoo | Farm |
|------|------------|------|
| | | |
| | | |
| | | |
| | | |
| | | |
| | | |
| | | |
| | | |
| | | |
| | | |

# Answers

**Commonly Mistaken Hiragana (page 85)** **Part A** 1. く 2. あ 3. さ 4. た 5. ぬ 6. ね 7. わ 8. ま 9. す 10. り 11. ら 12. け 13. そ 14. つ 15. に 16. は 17. や **Part B** 1. し 2. お 3. き 4. な 5. め 6. れ 7. ろ 8. ほ 9. む 10. る 11. う 12. せ 13. ち 14. て 15. の 16. も 17. え

**Commonly Mistaken Combined Characters (page 86)** **Part A** 1. しゅ 2. ちょ 3. みゅ 4. びゃ 5. ぎゅ 6. にゃ 7. りゃ 8. ぴゅ 9. じょ 10. きゃ 11. ひょ 12. ぴょ 13. きゅ 14. しょ 15. びょ **Part B** 1. じゅ 2. にょ 3. にゅ 4. ひゃ 5. みょ 6. びゅ 7. りょ 8. ひゅ 9. ちゅ 10. じゃ 11. ちゃ 12. りゅ 13. ぎゃ 14. しゃ 15. ぴゃ

**Map of Japan (page 87)** にほん (Japan), きた (North) 1. ほっかいどう 2. ほんしゅう 3. しこく 4. きゅうしゅう 5. おきなわ 6. さっぽろ 7. あおもり 8. せんだい 9. ながの 10. とうきょう 11. よこはま 12. なごや 13. こうべ 14. きょうと 15. おおさか 16. ひろしま 17. ふくおか

**Family Members (page 88)** 1. ぼく 2. おじいさん 3. わたし 4. おばあさん 5. いもうと 6. おとうさん 7. おとうと 8. おかあさん 9. おじさん 10. おにいさん 11. おばさん 12. おねえさん

**Daily Expressions (page 89)** <u>DOWN</u> 1. すみません 2. こんにちは 4. おげんきですか 5. おやすみなさい 6. ごめんなさい 10. どういたしまして 11. いいえ <u>ACROSS</u> 3. こんばんは 4. おはようございます 7. げんきです 8. さようなら 9. ありがとうございます 12. はい

**Numbers (page 90)** 9→18→27→37→46→56→55→64→63→73→72→81→91→ 92→83→73→74→75→84→94→85→75→76→67→57→47→37→28→39→30→20 →9 Finished! (Pictured: Map of Japan)

**Parts of the Body (page 91)** 1. あたま 2. かた 3. ひざ 4. あし 5. て 6. め 7. みみ 8. くち 9. はな 10. かみ 11. おなか 12. せなか 13. かお 14. は 15. のど 16. くび 17. てくび 18. あしくび 19. むね 20. うで 21. ゆび 22. つめ 23. ひじ 24. からだ

**Weather (page 92)** 1. てんき 2. はれ 3. あめ 4. くもり 5. ゆき 6. あらし 7. かぜがつよい 8. あつい 9. さむい

**Places at School (page 93)** 1. ようちえん 2. しょうがっこう 3. ちゅうがっこう 4. こうこう 5. だいがく 6. きょうしつ 7. ほけんしつ 8. としょしつ 9. おんがくしつ 10. しょくどう 11. うんどうじょう 12. たいいくかん 13. きょうしつ、としょしつ 14. だいがく、こうこう 15. としょしつ、ほけんしつ、おんがくしつ

**In the Classroom (page 94)** 1. えんぴつ 2. かみ 3. はさみ 4. ほん 5. のり 6. いす 7. つくえ 8. じょうぎ 9. でんたく 10. まど 11. でんき 12. とけい 13. かみ、のり、ほん、えんぴつ 14. いす、まど、でんき 15. とけい、でんたく、でんき

**At the Department Store (page 95)** 1. (6th) ろっかい 2. (10th) じゅっかい or じっかい 3. (4th) よんかい 4. (9th) きゅうかい 5. (B1) ちかいっかい 6. (1st) いっかい 7. (7th) ななかい 8. (2nd) にかい 9. (5th) ごかい 10. (3rd) さんがい

**Japanese Foods (page 96)** 1. ごはん 2. おにぎり 3. おべんとう 4. すし 5. さしみ 6. うどん 7. そば 8. ざるそば 9. やきそば 10. やきとり 11. てんぷら 12. やきいも

**Japanese Lunch Kiosk (page 97)** 1. 500 えん 2. 130 えん 3. 350 えん 4. 400 えん 5. 200 えん 6. 600 えん 7. 650 えん 8. 550 えん

**Animals (page 98)** Pets (いぬ、とり、かめ、きんぎょ、ねこ、かえる) Zoo (へび、きりん、さる、とら、くま、ぞう、きつね、わに、しか、りす) Farm (うし、うさぎ、にわとり、ひつじ、ぶた、うま)

# SECTION FOUR
# The Basic 46 Katakana Characters

| | | | | |
|---|---|---|---|---|
| a ア | i イ | u ウ | e エ | o オ |
| ka カ | ki キ | ku ク | ke ケ | ko コ |
| sa サ | shi シ | su ス | se セ | so ソ |
| ta タ | chi チ | tsu ツ | te テ | to ト |
| na ナ | ni ニ | nu ヌ | ne ネ | no ノ |
| ha (wa)* ハ | hi ヒ | fu フ | he (e)* ヘ | ho ホ |
| ma マ | mi ミ | mu ム | me メ | mo モ |
| ya ヤ | | yu ユ | | yo ヨ |
| ra ラ | ri リ | ru ル | re レ | ro ロ |
| wa ワ | | | | o** ヲ |
| n ン | | | | |

* These characters are pronounced differently when they are used as grammatical particles.
** This character is only used as a grammatical particle. It is not used to write words.

THE BASIC 46 KATAKANA CHARACTERS

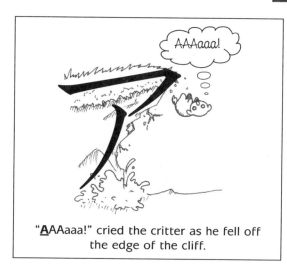

"**a**" as in f**a**ther

"**A**AAaaa!" cried the critter as he fell off the edge of the cliff.

**Writing Tip** "**a**" has two strokes and both are brushes.

Trace these characters.

Write the character in the boxes below, and then circle the one you think is best.

1. **a me ri ka** (America; United States)

2. **su ko a** (score)

3. **e a ko n** (air conditioner; air conditioning)

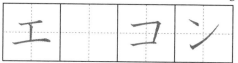

4. **ā to** (art)

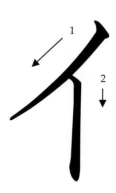

"i" as in <u>ea</u>sy

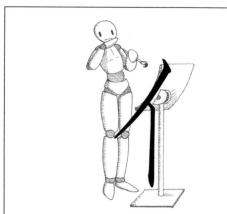

An <u>ea</u>sel holds your picture while you work on it or display it.

**Writing Tip** "i" has two strokes: 1) a brush and 2) stop.

Trace these characters.

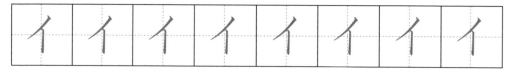

Write the character in the boxes below, and then circle the one you think is best.

1. **to i re** (toilet)

2. **a i ro n** (iron)

3. **na i fu** (knife)

4. **i gi ri su** (England)

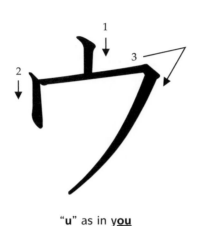

"u" as in y**ou**

"**Oo**oo!" The water balloon was cold as it splashed on his back!

**Writing Tip** "u" has three strokes: 1) a stop, 2) stop and 3) brush.

Trace these characters.

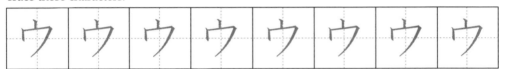

Write the character in the boxes below, and then circle the one you think is best.

1. **u i ru su** ((computer) virus)

2. **ki u i** (kiwi)

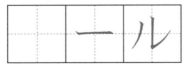

3. **ma u su** ((computer) mouse)

4. **ū ru** (wool)

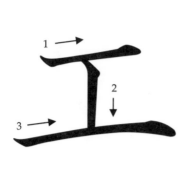

"**e**" as in r<u>e</u>d

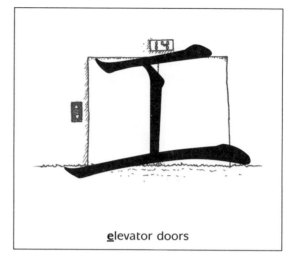

<u>e</u>levator doors

**Writing Tip** "e" has three strokes and they are all stops.

Trace these characters.

Write the character in the boxes below, and then circle the one you think is best.

1. **u ē tā** (waiter)

2. **e rā** ((computer) error)

3. **e su sa i zu** (small; "S" size)

4. **e i zu** (AIDS)

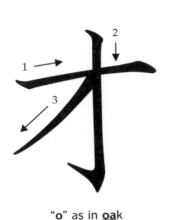

"o" as in <u>oa</u>k

an <u>O</u>lympic figure skater

**Writing Tip** "o" has three strokes: 1) a stop, 2) jump and 3) brush.

Trace these characters.

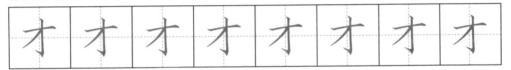

Write the character in the boxes below, and then circle the one you think is best.

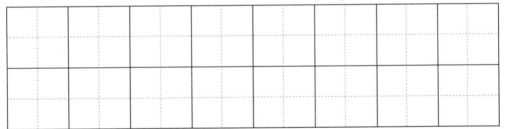

1. **o re n ji** (orange)

2. **ta o ru** (towel)

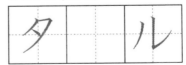

3. **o ru gan** (organ – musical instrument)

4. **o i ru** (oil)

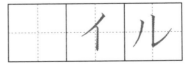

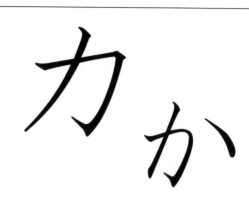

"**ka**" as in <u>ca</u>r

Katakana "**ka**" カ and hiragana "*ka*" か look alike, except that katakana "**ka**" has one fewer stroke, and its lines are straighter and more angular.

**Writing Tip** "ka" has two strokes: 1) a jump and 2) brush.

Trace these characters.

Write the character in the boxes below, and then circle the one you think is best.

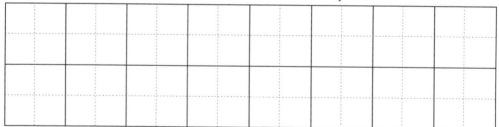

1. **ka me ra** (camera)

2. **ka ra o ke** (karaoke)

3. **ka ta ka na** (katakana characters)

4. **ka na da** (Canada)

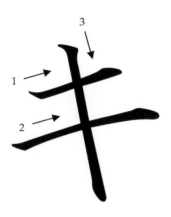

"ki" as in <u>key</u>

Katakana "**ki**" キ and hiragana "**ki**" き look alike, except that katakana "**ki**" has one fewer stroke, and it does not have a "jump" stroke.

**Writing Tip** "ki" has three strokes and they are all stops.

Trace these characters.

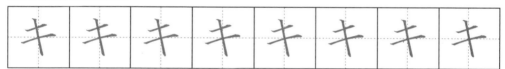

Write the character in the boxes below, and then circle the one you think is best.

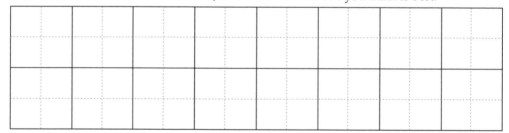

1. **su tē ki** (steak)

2. **me ki shi ko** (Mexico)

3. **ho chi ki su** (stapler – Hotchkiss)

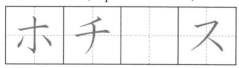

4. **su ki i** (ski; skiing)

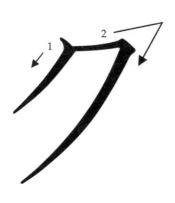

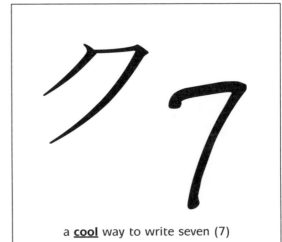

"**ku**" as in cuc<u>koo</u>

a <u>**cool**</u> way to write seven (7)

**Writing Tip** "ku" has two strokes and both are brushes.

Trace these characters.

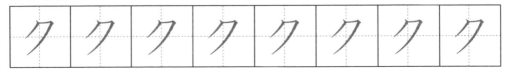

Write the character in the boxes below, and then circle the one you think is best.

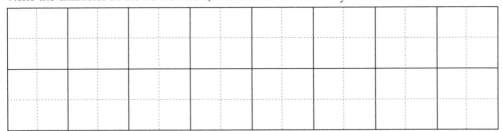

1. **pi n ku** (pink)

2. **ku ra su** (class)

3. **ta ku shi i** (taxi)

4. **ba i ku** (motorcycle)

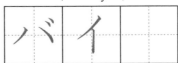

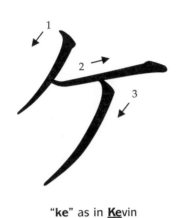

"**ke**" as in **Ke**vin

a **ka**ngaroo

**Writing Tip** "**ke**" has three strokes: 1) a brush, 2) stop and 3) brush.

Trace these characters.

| ケ | ケ | ケ | ケ | ケ | ケ | ケ | ケ |
|---|---|---|---|---|---|---|---|

Write the character in the boxes below, and then circle the one you think is best.

| | | | | | | | |
|---|---|---|---|---|---|---|---|
| | | | | | | | |

1. **su ke bō** (skateboard; to skateboard)

| ス | | ボ | ー |
|---|---|---|---|

2. **kē ki** (cake)

| | ー | キ |
|---|---|---|

3. **su kē to** (skates; to skate)

| ス | | ー | ト |
|---|---|---|---|

4. **ke ni a** (Kenya)

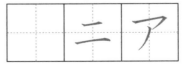

| | ニ | ア |
|---|---|---|

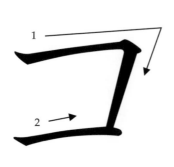

"**ko**" as in <u>co</u>coa

a cup of hot <u>co</u>coa

**Writing Tip** "ko" has two strokes and both are stops.

Trace these characters.

Write the character in the boxes below, and then circle the one you think is best.

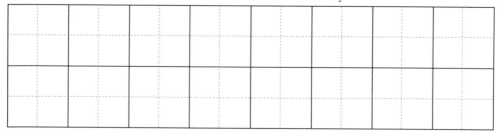

1. **ko n sā to** (concert)

2. **kō chi** (coach)

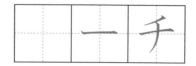

3. **kō hii** (coffee)

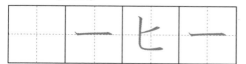

4. **kō to** (coat; (tennis) court)

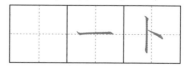

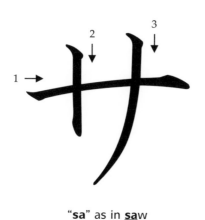

"**sa**" as in <u>sa</u>w

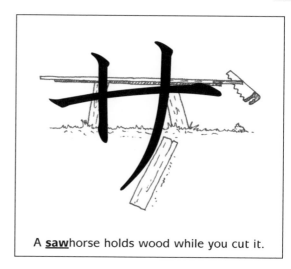

A <u>saw</u>horse holds wood while you cut it.

**Writing Tip** "**sa**" has three strokes: 1) a stop, 2) stop and 3) brush.

Trace these characters.

Write the character in the boxes below, and then circle the one you think is best.

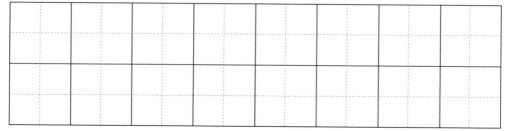

1. **sa i n** (signature; autograph)

2. **sā ka su** (circus)

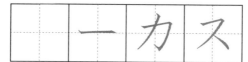

3. **sā chi** (search)

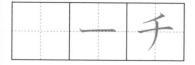

4. **sa n da ru** (sandals)

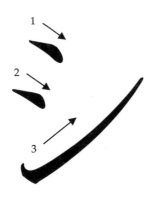

"shi" as in <u>she</u>

<u>She</u> tilted her head and smiled.

**Writing Tip** "shi" has three strokes: 1) a stop, 2) stop and 3) brush.

Trace these characters.

Write the character in the boxes below, and then circle the one you think is best.

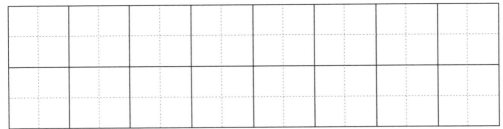

1. **shi ri a** (Syria)

2. **mi shi n** (sewing machine)

3. **shi ri a ru** (cereal)

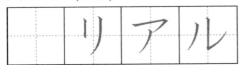

"**su**" as in **su**per

It's **Su**perman... er, super-critter.

**Writing Tip** "su" has two strokes: 1) a brush and 2) stop.

Trace these characters.

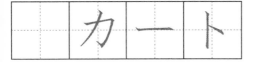

Write the character in the boxes below, and then circle the one you think is best.

1. **su kā to** (skirt)

2. **su te re o** (stereo)

3. **ku ri su ma su** (Christmas)

4. **ki su** (kiss)

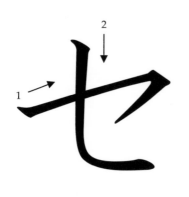

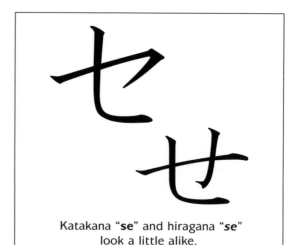

"**se**" as in s<u>e</u>t

Katakana "**se**" and hiragana "*se*" look a little alike.

**Writing Tip** "se" has two strokes: 1) a brush and 2) stop.

Trace these characters.

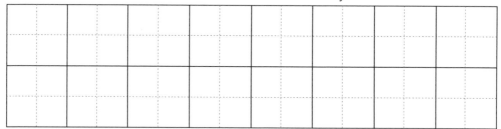

Write the character in the boxes below, and then circle the one you think is best.

1. s**ē tā** (sweater)

2. s**ē ru** (sale)

3. **se ro ri** (celery)

4. **se i kō** (Seiko watch corporation)

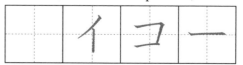

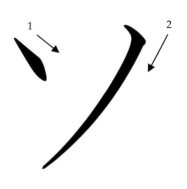

1   2

"so" as in <u>so</u>

A kid (goat) got into a fight after school, and he got an eye knocked out! The next day when other kids (goats) pointed and said, "You've only got one eye," he said, "<u>So</u>!"

**Writing Tip** "so" has two strokes: 1) a stop and 2) brush.

Trace these characters.

Write the character in the boxes below, and then circle the one you think is best.

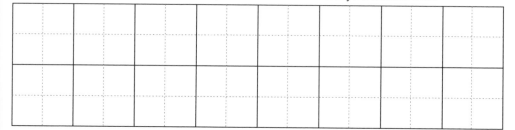

1. **shi i sō** (seesaw)

2. **so fa** (sofa)

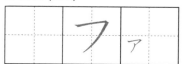

3. **so u ru** (Seoul, Korea; soul)

4. **sō da** (soda)

## READING PRACTICE 1: ア ~ ソ

You should be able to read the words below now. Fold the page lengthwise (or cover it with your hand) so you can only see the katakana words on the left hand side. Try reading them aloud and then check with the words on the right. Keep practicing until you can read them all. For an extra challenge try reading the Japanese and saying the English word before checking.

**Note:** In katakana long vowels are written with a line (ー) called **bō**, rather than writing one of the five vowels as in hiragana. In this way, katakana writing is simpler than hiragana writing. Several of the example words below have long vowels. In order to improve your pronunciation, be sure to pronounce the long vowels with approximately twice the length of a single syllable.

| | | | | |
|---|---|---|---|---|
| ア | イ | ス | | **a i su** (ice) |
| ス | コ | ア | | **su ko a** (score) |
| ア | ク | セ | ス | **a ku se su** (access) |
| イ | カ | | | **i ka** (squid) |
| サ | イ | | | **sa i** (rhino) |
| キ | ウ | イ | | **ki u i** (kiwi) |
| エ | キ | ス | | **e ki su** (extract) |
| オ | ス | カ | ー | **o su kā** (the Oscar) |
| オ | ア | シ | ス | **o a shi su** (oasis) |
| サ | ー | カ | ス | **sā ka su** (circus) |
| キ | ス | | | **ki su** (kiss) |
| ス | イ | ス | | **su i su** (Switzerland) |
| カ | ー | キ | | **kā ki** (khaki color) |
| ス | キ | ー | | **su ki i** (to ski; skiing) |
| サ | ク | セ | ス | **sa ku se su** (success) |
| ケ | ー | キ | | **kē ki** (cake) |
| オ | ー | ケ | ー | **ō kē** (okay) |
| コ | コ | ア | | **ko ko a** (cocoa) |
| セ | イ | コ | ー | **se i kō** (Seiko company) |
| シ | ー | ソ | ー | **shi i sō** (seesaw) |
| コ | ソ | コ | ソ | **ko so ko so** (sneakily; stealthily) |

Romaji pronunciation guide:

| | |
|---|---|
| *a* | as in **father** |
| *i* | as in **easy** |
| *u* | as in **you** |
| *e* | as in **red** |
| *o* | as in **oak** |

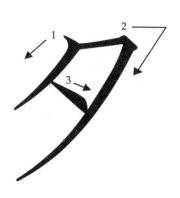

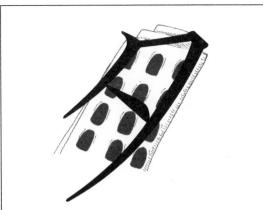

"ta" as in t**a**ll

the leaning **tower** of Pisa (In Japanese "tower" is pronounced with a "**ta**" as in t**a**ll).

**Writing Tip** "**ta**" has tree strokes: 1) a brush, 2) brush and 3) stop.

Trace these characters.

Write the character in the boxes below, and then circle the one you think is best.

**1. ta i** (Thailand; tie)

**2. sē tā** (sweater)

**3. ta ku shi i** (taxi)

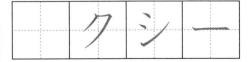

**4. ta ko su** (taco)

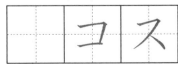

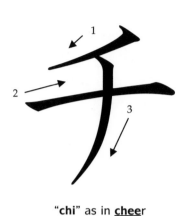

"chi" as in <u>chee</u>r

a <u>chee</u>rleader

**Writing Tip** "chi" has three strokes: 1) a brush, 2) stop and 3) brush.

Trace these characters.

Write the character in the boxes below, and then circle the one you think is best.

1. **chi ki n** ((cooked) chicken)

2. **se n chi** (centimeter)

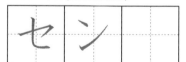

3. **i n chi** (inch)

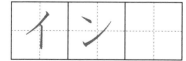

4. **kō chi** (coach)

"tsu" as in ca**ts**

**Two** children are sliding down a slide.
("**ts**" like ca**ts** and "**u**" like y**ou**)

**Writing Tip** "**tsu**" has three strokes: 1) a stop 2) stop and 3) brush. (Note: tsu ツ and shi シ look alike, but the strokes in **tsu** go downward, and the strokes in **shi** go more to the right.)

Trace these characters.

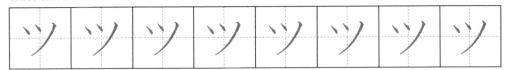

Write the character in the boxes below, and then circle the one you think is best.

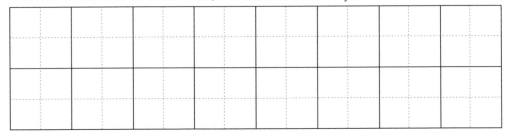

1. **sū tsu** (suit)

2. **tsu ā** (tour)

3. **shi i tsu** ((bed)sheet)

4. **ta i tsu** (tights)

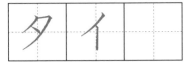

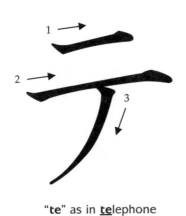

"**te**" as in **te**lephone

a **te**lephone pole and wires

**Writing Tip** "**te**" has three strokes: 1) a stop, 2) stop and 3) brush

Trace these characters.

Write the character in the boxes below, and then circle the one you think is best.

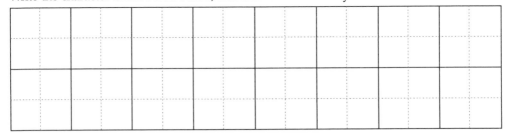

1. **kā te n** (curtains)

2. **te ki su to** (textbook)

3. **te ku** (tech – abbr.)

4. **ā ki te ku to** (architect)

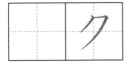

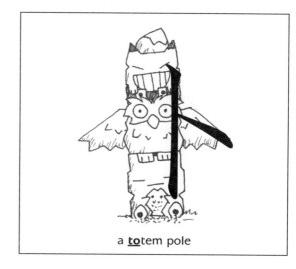

"**to**" as in **to**tem

a **to**tem pole

**Writing Tip** "to" has two strokes and they are both stops.

Trace these characters.

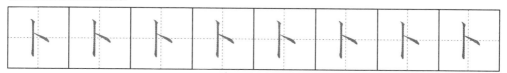

Write the character in the boxes below, and then circle the one you think is best.

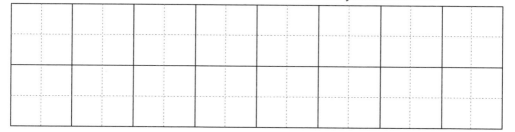

1. **su kā to** (skirt)

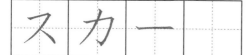

2. **te su to** (test)

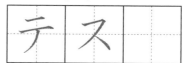

3. **sa i to** ((web or real) site)

4. **su tā to** (start)

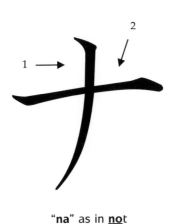

"**na**" as in **no**t

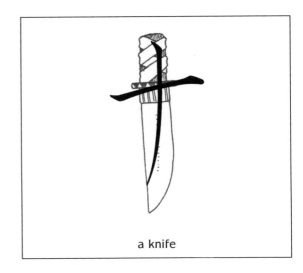

a knife

**Writing Tip** "**na**" has two strokes: 1) a stop and 2) brush.

Trace these characters.

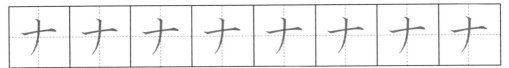

Write the character in the boxes below, and then circle the one you think is best.

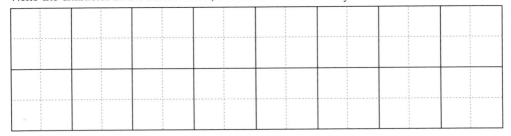

1. **na i fu** (knife)

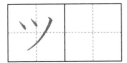

2. **na rē tā** (narrator)

3. **tsu na** (tuna)

4. **sa u na** (sauna)

5. **na sa** (NASA)

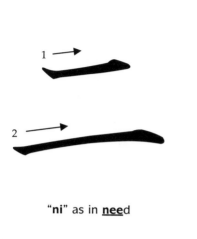

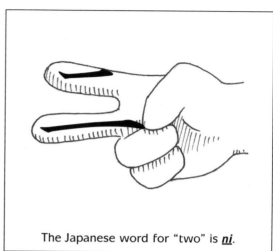

"ni" as in **nee**d

The Japanese word for "two" is **_ni_**.

**Writing Tip** "ni" has two strokes and they are both stops.

Trace these characters.

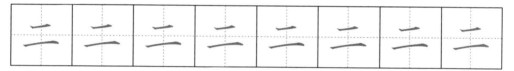

Write the character in the boxes below, and then circle the one you think is best.

1. **te ni su** (tennis)

2. **e su to ni a** (Estonia)

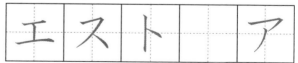

3. **so ni i** (Sony company)

4. **su ni i kā** (sneakers)

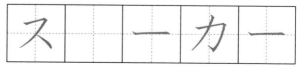

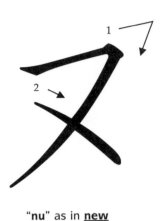

"nu" as in <u>new</u>

a <u>new</u> way to write seven (7)

**Writing Tip** "nu" has two strokes: 1) a brush and 2) stop.

Trace these characters.

Write the character in the boxes below, and then circle the one you think is best.

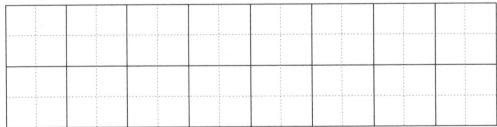

1. **a i nu** (Ainu – indigenous people of Japan)

2. **su nū pi i** (Snoopy)

3. **nū do ru** (noodles)

4. **ka nū** (canoe)

"**ne**" as in **ne**st

a **ne**st on top of a tree

**Writing Tip** "**ne**" has four strokes: 1) a stop, 2) brush, 3) stop and 4) stop.

Trace these characters.

Write the character in the boxes below, and then circle the one you think is best.

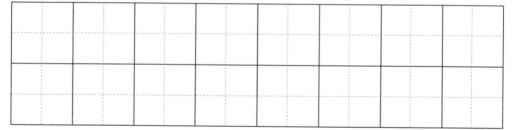

1. **i n tā ne tto** (internet)

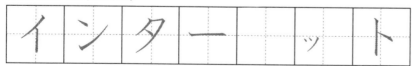

2. **ne ga** ((photo) negatives)  3. **to n ne ru** (tunnel)

"**no**" as in **no**se

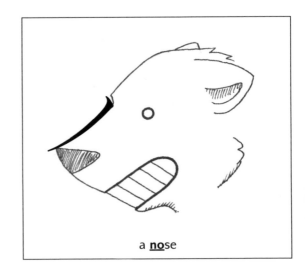

a **no**se

**Writing Tip** "**no**" has only one stroke and it is a brush.

Trace these characters.

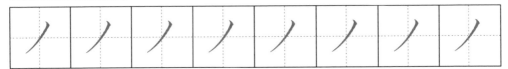

Write the character in the boxes below, and then circle the one you think is best.

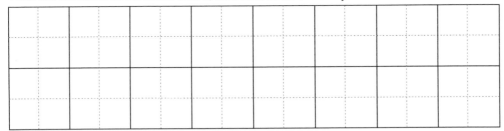

1. **nō to** (notebook)

2. **pi a no** (piano)

3. **ka ji no** (casino)

4. **su nō bō do** (snowboard; snowboarding)

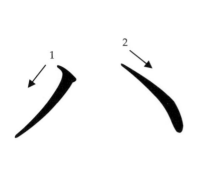

"**ha**" as in **ha**wk

the two wings of a fearsome **ha**wk
(or a slightly dazed-looking hawk)

**Writing Tip** "**ha**" has two strokes: 1) a brush and 2) stop

Trace these characters.

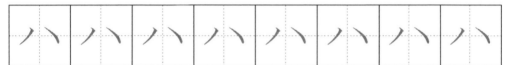

Write the character in the boxes below, and then circle the one you think is best.

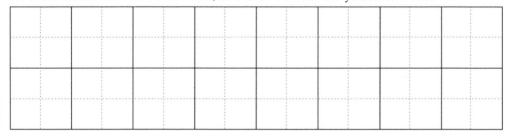

1. **ha i ki n gu** (hiking)

2. **ha i chi** (Haiti)

3. **ha i te ku** (high tech)

4. **ha su ki i** (Husky – dog)

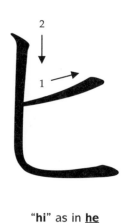

"**hi**" as in <u>he</u>

<u>He</u> drives the car.

**Writing Tip** "**hi**" has two strokes and they are both stops.

Trace these characters.

Write the character in the boxes below, and then circle the one you think is best.

1. **kō hi i** (coffee)

2. **hi n to** (hint)

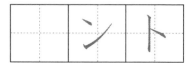

3. **hi i tā** (heater)

4. **hi i rō** (hero)

"**fu**" as in **Hoot!**
(except the lips are less rounded,
and more air escapes from the mouth)

The owl cries, "**Hoot**! **Hoot**!"

**Writing Tip** "fu" has only one stroke and it is a brush.

Trace these characters.

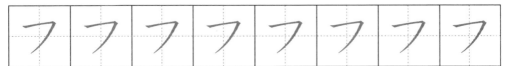

Write the character in the boxes below, and then circle the one you think is best.

1. **su kā fu** (scarf)

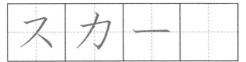

2. **fu ra n su** (France)

3. **so fu to** (software)

4. **go ru fu** (golf)

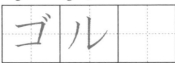

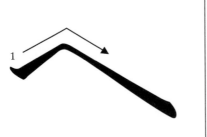

1

"he" as in <u>he</u>lp

There are no significant differences between katakana "**he**" and hiragana "*he*."

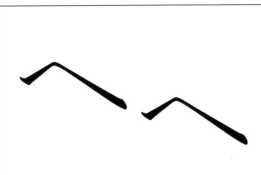

**Writing Tip** "he" has only one stroke and it is a stop.

Trace these characters.

Write the character in the boxes below, and then circle the one you think is best.

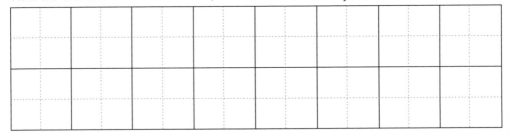

1. **he ri** (helicopter)

2. **he ddo ho n** (headphones)

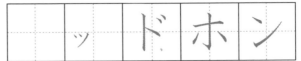

3. **he ru pu** (help)

4. **he a ka rā** (hair dye; hair coloring)

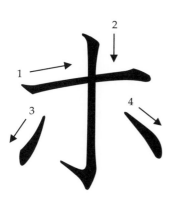

"**ho**" as in <u>**Ho**</u>! <u>**Ho**</u>!

Mr. "<u>**Ho Ho**</u>" laughs even when stuck in a chimney!

**Writing Tip** "ho" has four strokes: 1) a stop, 2) jump, 3) stop and 4) stop.

Trace these characters.

Write the character in the boxes below, and then circle the one you think is best.

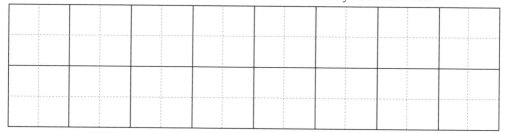

1. **ho te ru** (hotel)

2. **ho kkē** (hockey)

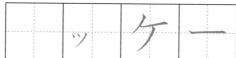

3. **hō mu** ((train station) platform)

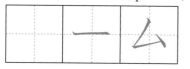

4. **ho i ru** (foil)

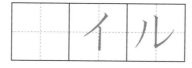

## READING PRACTICE 2: タ ～ ホ

You should be able to read the words below now. Fold the page lengthwise (or cover it with your hand) so you can only see the katakana words on the left hand side. Try reading them aloud and then check with the words on the right. Keep practicing until you can read them all. For an extra challenge try reading the Japanese and saying the English word before checking.

**Note:** In katakana long vowels are written with a line (ー) called **bō**, rather than writing one of the five vowels as in hiragana. In this way, katakana writing is simpler than hiragana writing. Several of the example words below have long vowels. In order to improve your pronunciation, be sure to pronounce the long vowels with approximately twice the length of a single syllable.

| Katakana | Romaji (English) |
|---|---|
| タ ク シ ー | **ta ku shi i** (taxi) |
| タ コ ス | **ta ko su** (taco) |
| コ ー チ | **kō chi** (coach) |
| ス ー ツ | **sū tsu** (suit) |
| ツ ア ー | **tsu ā** (tour) |
| テ キ ス ト | **te ki su to** (textbook) |
| ス カ ー ト | **su kā to** (skirt) |
| テ ス ト | **te su to** (test) |
| ナ イ フ | **na i fu** (knife) |
| ツ ナ | **tsu na** (tuna) |
| カ タ カ ナ | **ka ta ka na** (katakana) |
| テ ニ ス | **te ni su** (tennis) |
| ス ニ ー カ ー | **su ni i kā** (sneakers) |
| カ ヌ ー | **ka nū** (canoe) |
| ア イ ヌ | **a i nu** (Ainu – indigenous people of northern Japan) |
| ノ ー ト | **nō to** (notebook) |
| ハ ス キ ー | **ha su ki i** (Husky – dog) |
| コ ー ヒ ー | **kō hi i** (coffee) |
| ヒ ン ト | **hi n to** (hint) |
| ソ フ ト | **so fu to** (software) |

| Romaji pronunciation guide: | |
|---|---|
| *a* | as in **father** |
| *i* | as in **easy** |
| *u* | as in **you** |
| *e* | as in **red** |
| *o* | as in **oak** |

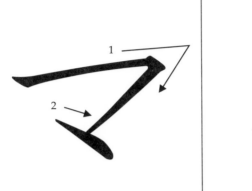

"**ma**" as in <u>mo</u>m

<u>Mo</u>m holds Baby while
she attends to some work.

**Writing Tip** "**ma**" has two strokes: 1) a brush and 2) stop.

Trace these characters.

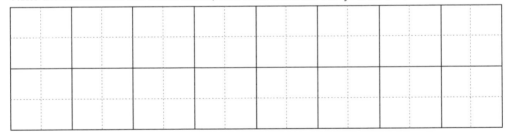

Write the character in the boxes below, and then circle the one you think is best.

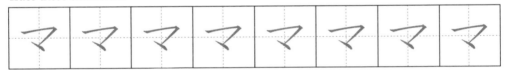

1. **to ma to** (tomato)

2. **mā kā** (marker)

3. **ma i ku** (microphone)

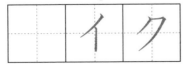

4. **ma i ru** (mile)

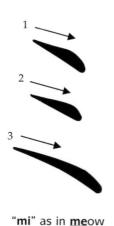

"**mi**" as in <u>me</u>ow

A cat's three whiskers, "<u>Me</u>ow!"

**Writing Tip** "mi" has three strokes and all three are stops.

Trace these characters.

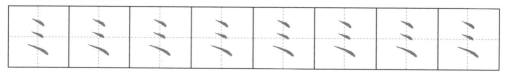

Write the character in the boxes below, and then circle the one you think is best.

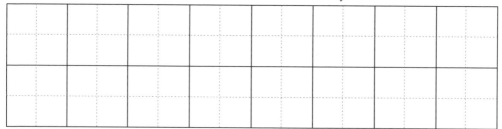

1. **mi ki sā** (blender)

2. **sa ra mi** (salami)

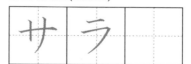

3. **mi ni kā** (toy car)

4. **mi i ra** (mummy; from Portuguese)

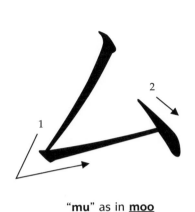

"mu" as in <u>moo</u>

I love ja<u>mu</u> (jam)!

**Writing Tip** "mu" has two strokes and both are stops.

Trace these characters.

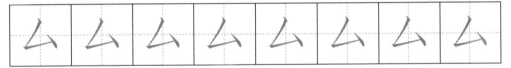

Write the character in the boxes below, and then circle the one you think is best.

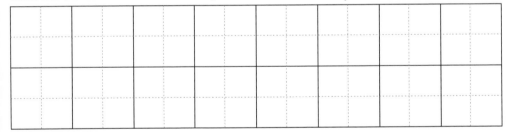

1. **chi i mu** (team)

2. **ha mu su tā** (hamster)

3. **hō mu su te i** (home stay)

"me" as in <u>Me</u>xico

the "X" in <u>Me</u>xico

**Writing Tip** "me" has two strokes: 1) a brush and 2) stop.

Trace these characters.

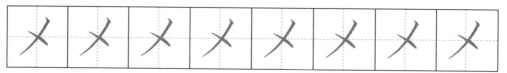

Write the character in the boxes below, and then circle the one you think is best.

**1. me ki shi ko** (Mexico)

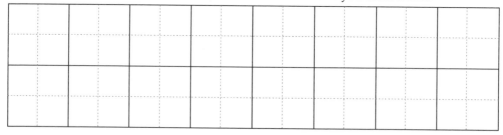

**2. mē to ru** (meter)

**3. a ni me** (Japanese cartoons)

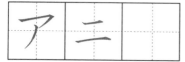

**4. me mo** (memo; notes)

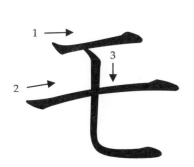

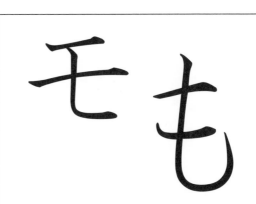

"**mo**" as in <u>mo</u>re

Hiragana "**mo**" and katakana "**mo**" look a bit alike. Note that stroke #3 does not go through stroke #1.

**Writing Tip** "mo" has three strokes and they are all stops.

Trace these characters.

Write the character in the boxes below, and then circle the one you think is best.

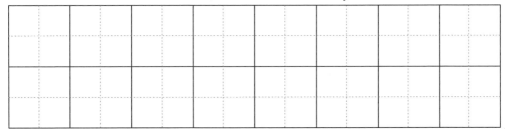

1. **sā mo n** (salmon – fish)

2. **shi na mo n** (cinnamon)

3. **mo ni tā** (monitor)

4. **mō ru** (mall)

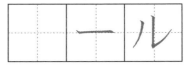

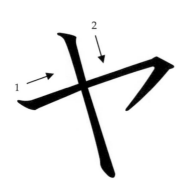

"**ya**" as in **ya**rn

Katakana "**ya**" and hiragana "**ya**" look a bit alike.

**Writing Tip** "ya" has two strokes: 1) a brush and 2) stop.

Trace these characters.

Write the character in the boxes below, and then circle the one you think is best.

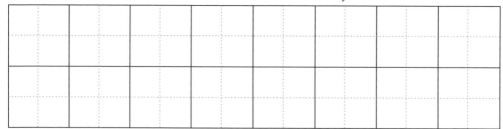

1. **ta i ya** (tire)

2. **i ya ho n** (earphones)

3. **da i ya** (diamond)

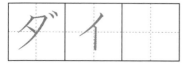

4. **ya fū** (Yahoo – company)

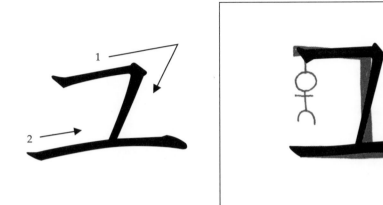

"yu" as in **you**

**You** won the "hangman" game!

**Writing Tip** "**yu**" has two strokes and both are stops.

Trace these characters.

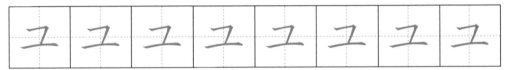

Write the character in the boxes below, and then circle the one you think is best.

1. **yū tā n** (u-turn)

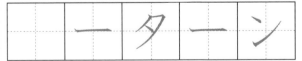

2. **yū ro** (Euro)

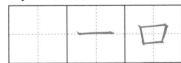

3. **yū mo a** (humor)

4. **yū zā** (user)

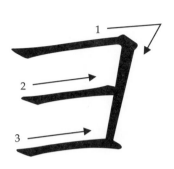

"**yo**" as in **yo**gurt

**yo**gurt

**Writing Tip** "yo" has three strokes and they are all stops.

Trace these characters.

Write the character in the boxes below, and then circle the one you think is best.

1. **ku re yo n** (crayon)

2. **to yo ta** (Toyota – company)

3. **yō yō** (yo-yo)

4. **yō ga** (yoga)

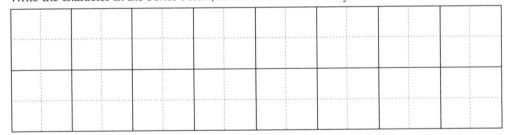

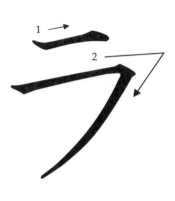

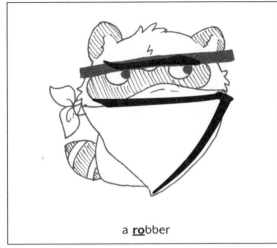

"**ra**" as in **ro**bber

a **ro**bber

**Writing Tip** "ra" has two strokes: 1) a stop and 2) brush.

Trace these characters.

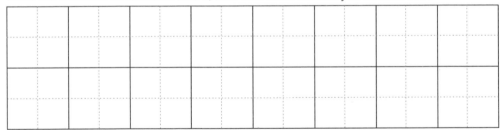

Write the character in the boxes below, and then circle the one you think is best.

1. **ka me ra** (camera )

2. **ku ra su** (school class)

3. **hō mu ra n** (homerun)

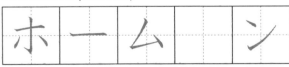

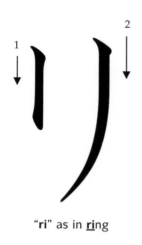

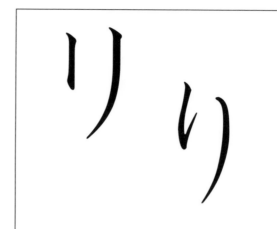

"**ri**" as in <u>ri</u>ng

Katakana "**ri**" and hiragana "***ri***" look a bit alike.

**Writing Tip** "ri" has two strokes: 1) a stop and 2) brush.

Trace these characters.

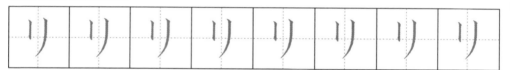

Write the character in the boxes below, and then circle the one you think is best.

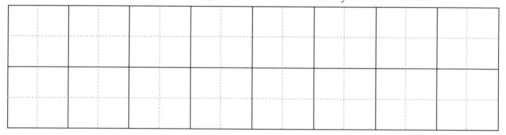

1. **a fu ri ka** (Africa)

2. **i ta ri a** (Italy)

3. **a i su ku ri i mu** (ice cream)

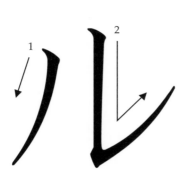

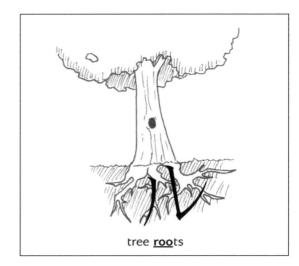

"ru" as in **roo**ts

tree **roo**ts

**Writing Tip** "ru" has two strokes and both are brushes.

Trace these characters.

Write the character in the boxes below, and then circle the one you think is best.

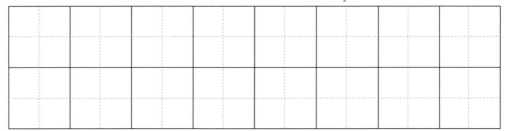

1. **ho te ru** (hotel)

2. **mi ru ku** ((cow's) milk)

3. **a ru mi ho i ru** (aluminum foil)

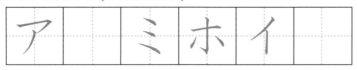

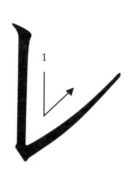

"**re**" as in **ra**in

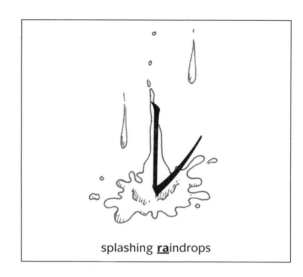

splashing **ra**indrops

**Writing Tip** "**re**" has one stroke: a brush.

Trace these characters.

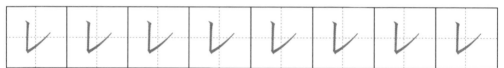

Write the character in the boxes below, and then circle the one you think is best.

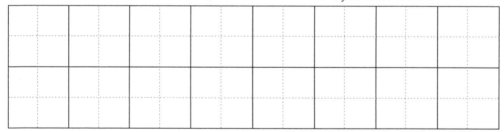

1. **re su to ra n** (restaurant)

2. **re shi i to** (receipt)

3. **e re ki** (electric guitar)  4. **ka rē ra i su** (curry rice)

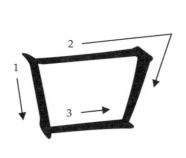

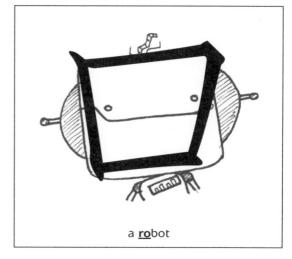

"**ro**" as in **ro**bot

a **ro**bot

**Writing Tip** "ro" has three strokes and all three are stops.

Trace these characters.

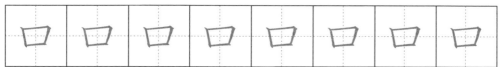

Write the character in the boxes below, and then circle the one you think is best.

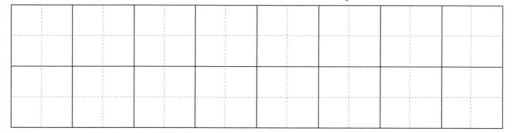

1. **ki ro** (kilogram; kilometer)    2. **su to rō** (drinking straw)

    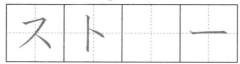

3. **te ro** (terrorism)    4. **ro shi a** (Russia)

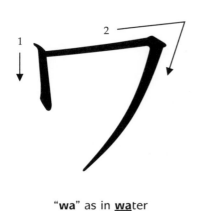

"**wa**" as in **wa**ter

"I **wa**nt a cookie!"

**Writing Tip** "wa" has two strokes: 1) a stop and 2) brush.

Trace these characters.

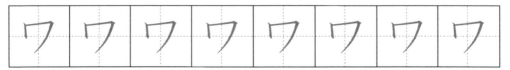

Write the character in the boxes below, and then circle the one you think is best.

1. **ha wa i** (Hawaii)

2. **wa i ya re su** (wireless)

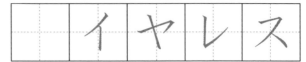

3. **wā ku shi i to** (worksheet)

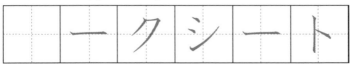

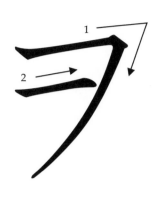

"**o**" as in <u>oa</u>k
(same pronunciation as オ)

"<u>**Oh**</u>, this cookie is <u>*oishii*</u> (delicious)!"

**Writing Tip** "o" has two strokes: 1) a brush and 2) stop.

Trace these characters.

Write the character in the boxes below, and then circle the one you think is best.

As a grammatical object marker, ヲ "o" is rarely used to write sentences, except in telegrams and some video games. Trace the light gray characters and write the character by yourself.

**su tā to bo ta n o  o shi te ku da sa i** (Push the start button.)

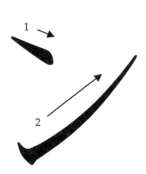

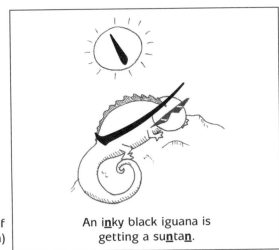

"n" as in i<u>n</u>k
(pronounced by touching the back of
the tongue to the roof of the mouth)

An i<u>n</u>ky black iguana is
getting a su<u>n</u>ta<u>n</u>.

**Writing Tip** "n" has two strokes: 1) a stop and 2) brush. (Note: ン "n" and ソ "so" look similar. A big difference is that "n" is written more from left to right, and "so" is written more from top to bottom.) Trace these characters.

Write the character in the boxes below, and then circle the one you think is best.

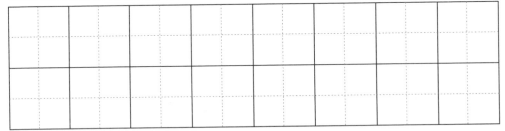

1. **me ro n** (melon)

2. **ma ra so n** (any running race)

3. **rā me n** (ramen noodles)

4. **mi shi n** (sewing machine)

## READING PRACTICE 3: マ ～ ン

You should be able to read the words below now. Cover the right hand side of the page so you can only see the katakana words on the left. Try reading them aloud, and then check with the romaji on the right hand side. Keep practicing until you can read them all. For an extra challenge try saying the English words before you check.

| Katakana | Romaji (English) |
| --- | --- |
| ト マ ト | **to ma to** (tomato) |
| マ イ ク | **ma i ku** (microphone) |
| ミ キ サ ー | **mi ki sā** (blender) |
| チ ー ム | **chi i mu** (team) |
| ホ ー ム ス テ イ | **hō mu su te i** (home stay) |
| ア ニ メ | **a ni me** (Japanese cartoons) |
| シ ナ モ ン | **shi na mo n** (cinnamon) |
| モ ニ タ ー | **mo ni tā** (monitor) |
| タ イ ヤ | **ta i ya** (tire) |
| イ ヤ ホ ン | **i ya ho n** (earphones) |
| ユ ー モ ア | **yū mo a** (humor) |
| ク レ ヨ ン | **ku re yo n** (crayon) |
| ヨ ー ヨ ー | **yō yō** (yo-yo) |
| カ メ ラ | **ka me ra** (camera) |
| ク ラ ス | **ku ra su** (school class) |
| ア イ ス ク リ ー ム | **a i su ku ri i mu** (ice cream) |
| ホ テ ル | **ho te ru** (hotel) |
| ミ ル ク | **mi ru ku** (cow's milk) |
| レ ス ト ラ ン | **re su to ran** (restaurant) |
| レ シ ー ト | **re shi i to** (receipt) |
| ス ト ロ ー | **su to rō** (drinking straw) |
| キ ロ | **ki ro** (kilogram; kilometer) |
| ワ ー ク シ ー ト | **wā ku shi i to** (worksheet) |
| ワ イ ヤ レ ス | **wa i ya re su** (wireless) |
| メ ロ ン | **me ro n** (melon) |
| ラ ー メ ン | **rā me n** (ramen noodles) |
| ミ シ ン | **mi shi n** (sewing machine) |
| マ ラ ソ ン | **ma ra so n** (any running race) |

Romaji pronunciation guide:
*a*   as in f**a**ther
*i*   as in **ea**sy
*u*   as in y**ou**
*e*   as in r**e**d
*o*   as in **oa**k

# SECTION FIVE
# Katakana Usage Rules

Katakana has a few basic rules to keep in mind. This section introduces the four katakana rules with simple explanations and many useful example words. Pay close attention to these example words; they will illustrate the rules and make them easier to understand and remember.

Although some of the rules are the same as hiragana, katakana has different uses than hiragana so its rules are a bit different too. First, the hiragana rule for changing the pronunciation of は, へ, and を when using them as grammatical particles does not apply to katakana since katakana characters are not used as particles (except in telegraphs, video games, and so on). Second, instead of the complicated rule for making long vowels in hiragana, you simply add a long dash ー called a **chōon** (long vowel) mark in katakana. For example, "cake" is written ケーキ (**kē ki**) with a **chōon** mark after the ケ (**ke**).

Katakana has one new rule that describes how to make 33 additional syllables for writing foreign words (see Rule 4). As you master the four rules of katakana usage you will be able to write any katakana word you like. After this chapter all you will need is practice, and you will be a proficient reader and writer of katakana.

## RULE 1 TENTEN ( ゛ ) AND MARU ( ゜ )

The first katakana rule describes how certain characters change pronunciations when the marks called **tenten** ( ゛ ) and **maru** ( ゜ ) are added to them. There are 18 characters that take the tenten ( ゛ ) mark, and there are 5 characters that take the **maru** ( ゜ ) mark. The chart below summarizes the changes when these marks are added.

## 23 Tenten and Maru Characters

| | | | | |
|---|---|---|---|---|
| ga ガ | gi ギ | gu グ | ge ゲ | go ゴ |
| za ザ | ji ジ | zu ズ | ze ゼ | zo ゾ |
| da ダ | | | de デ | do ド |
| ba バ | bi ビ | bu ブ | be ベ | bo ボ |
| pa パ | pi ピ | pu プ | pe ペ | po ポ |

Trace the gray characters and marks, and try writing them on your own in the blank boxes.

| | | | | | | | |
|---|---|---|---|---|---|---|---|
| ガ ga | ガ | ガ | | | | | |
| ギ gi | ギ | ギ | | | | | |
| グ gu | グ | グ | | | | | |
| ゲ ge | ゲ | ゲ | | | | | |
| ゴ go | ゴ | ゴ | | | | | |

1. **ga mu** (gum)

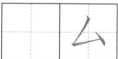

ム

2. **ga so ri n** (gasoline)

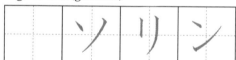

ソ リ ン

3. **a re ru gi i** (allergy)

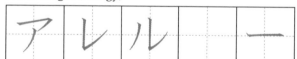

ア レ ル ー

4. **gi tā** (guitar)

タ ー

5. **sa n gu ra su** (sunglasses)

サ ン ラ ス

6. **gu rē** (grey)

レ ー

7. **gē mu** (game)

ー ム

8. **re ge e** (Reggae)

レ エ

9. *ke shi** **go mu** (eraser)

10. **go ru fu** (golf)

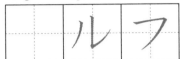

*hiragana

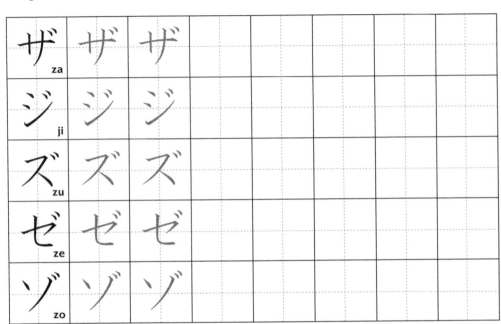

11. **ra za ni a** (lasagna)

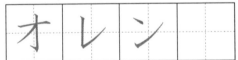

12. **rē zā** (laser)

13. **o re n ji** (orange)

14. **ra ji o** (radio)

15. **chi i zu** (cheese)

16. **ji i n zu** (jeans)

17. **gā ze** (gauze)

| ガ | ー | |
|---|---|---|

18. **zero** (zero)

| | ロ | |
|---|---|---|

19. **ze mi** (seminar)

| | ミ |
|---|---|

20. **ri zō to** (resort)

| リ | | ー | ト |
|---|---|---|---|

21. **a ma zo n** (Amazon)

| ア | マ | | ン |
|---|---|---|---|

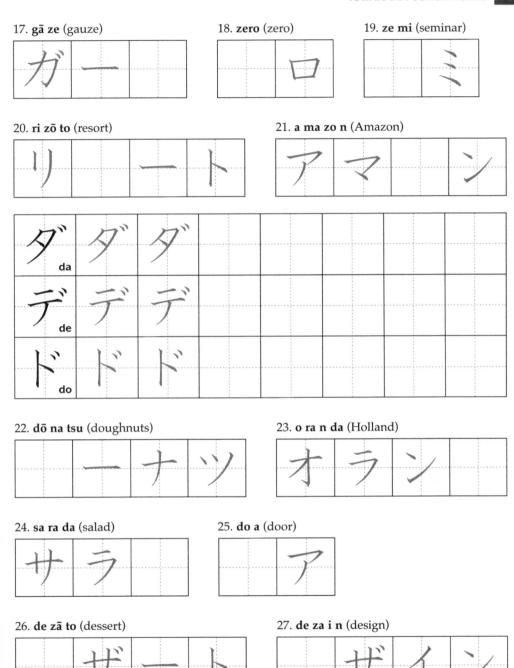

| ダ da | ダ | ダ | | | | |
|---|---|---|---|---|---|---|
| デ de | デ | デ | | | | |
| ド do | ド | ド | | | | |

22. **dō na tsu** (doughnuts)

| | ー | ナ | ツ |
|---|---|---|---|

23. **o ra n da** (Holland)

| オ | ラ | ン | |
|---|---|---|---|

24. **sa ra da** (salad)

| サ | ラ | |
|---|---|---|

25. **do a** (door)

| | ア |
|---|---|

26. **de zā to** (dessert)

| | ザ | ー | ト |
|---|---|---|---|

27. **de za i n** (design)

| | ザ | イ | ン |
|---|---|---|---|

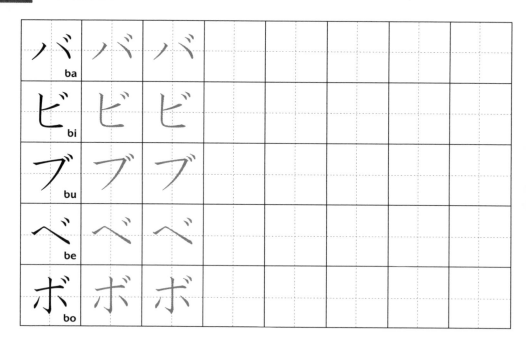

| バ ba | バ | バ | | | | | |
| ビ bi | ビ | ビ | | | | | |
| ブ bu | ブ | ブ | | | | | |
| ベ be | ベ | ベ | | | | | |
| ボ bo | ボ | ボ | | | | | |

28. **te re bi** (TV; television)

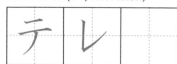

29. **ba su** (bus)

30. **ha n bā gā** (hamburger)

31. **be ru to** (belt)

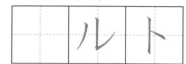

32. **zu bo n** (pants; trousers)

33. **ki i bō do** (keyboard)

**34. bu ra ji ru** (Brazil)

| | ラ | ジ | ル |
|---|---|---|---|

**35. tē bu ru** (table)

| テ | ー | | ル |
|---|---|---|---|

**36. i be n to** (event)

| イ | | ン | ト |
|---|---|---|---|

**37. ko n bi ni** (convenience store)

| コ | ン | | ニ |
|---|---|---|---|

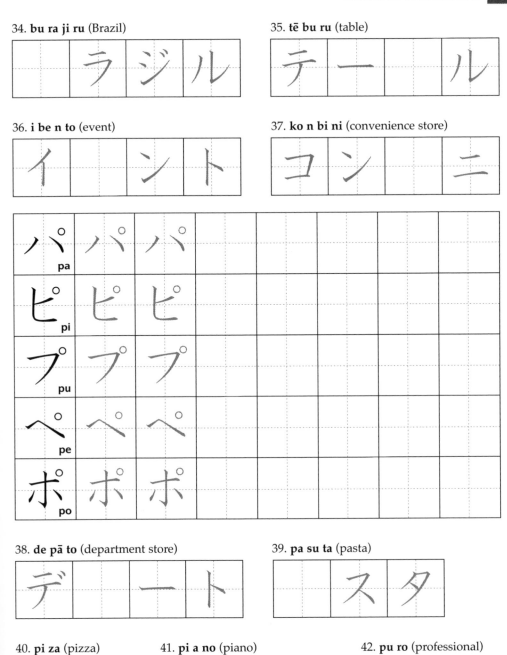

| パ pa | パ | パ | | | | | |
| ピ pi | ピ | ピ | | | | | |
| プ pu | プ | プ | | | | | |
| ペ pe | ペ | ペ | | | | | |
| ポ po | ポ | ポ | | | | | |

**38. de pā to** (department store)

| デ | | ー | ト |
|---|---|---|---|

**39. pa su ta** (pasta)

| | ス | タ |
|---|---|---|

**40. pi za** (pizza)

| | ザ |
|---|---|

**41. pi a no** (piano)

| | ア | ノ |
|---|---|---|

**42. pu ro** (professional)

| | ロ |
|---|---|

43. **pū ru** (pool)

44. **pu re ze n to** (present)

45. **su pe i n** (Spain)

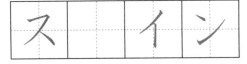

46. **pe n gi n** (penguin)

47. **su pō tsu** (sports)

48. **re pō to** (report)

## READING PRACTICE 4: TENTEN AND MARU

You should be able to read the words below now. Try covering the answers on the right hand side and reading the katakana words on the left. Try to guess the English meaning of each word before looking at the answers.

| | | | | | |
|---|---|---|---|---|---|
| ガ | ム | | | | **ga mu** (gum) |
| ギ | ター | ー | | | **gi tā** (guitar) |
| サ | ン | グ | ラ | ス | **sa n gu ra su** (sunglasses) |
| ゲ | ー | ム | | | **gē mu** (game) |
| ゴ | ル | フ | | | **go ru fu** (golf) |
| ラ | ザ | ニ | ア | | **ra za ni a** (lasagna) |
| チ | ー | ズ | | | **chi i zu** (cheese) |
| ゼ | ロ | | | | **ze ro** (zero) |
| リ | ゾ | ー | ト | | **ri zō to** (resort) |
| サ | ラ | ダ | | | **sa ra da** (salad) |
| デ | ザ | ー | ト | | **de zā to** (dessert) |
| ド | ア | | | | **do a** (door) |
| バ | ス | | | | **ba su** (bus) |
| テ | レ | ビ | | | **te re bi** (TV; television) |
| テ | ー | ブ | ル | | **tē bu ru** (table) |
| ベ | ル | ト | | | **be ru to** (belt) |
| キ | ー | ボ | ー | ド | **ki i bō do** (keyboard) |
| パ | ス | タ | | | **pa su ta** (pasta) |
| ピ | ア | ノ | | | **pi a no** (piano) |
| プ | ー | ル | | | **pū ru** (pool) |
| ス | ペ | イ | ン | | **su pe i n** (Spain) |
| ス | ポ | ー | ツ | | **su pō tsu** (sports) |

## RULE 2   COMBINED CHARACTERS

There are three special katakana characters that are used extensively in combination with 11 consonants to form 33 additional sounds. When combined in this way **"ya,"** **"yu"** and **"yo"** are written in half-size characters at the bottom left corner, as in the examples below. The chart below illustrates these 33 blended sounds, called **yō'on**.

### 33 Combined Characters

| | | | | | |
|---|---|---|---|---|---|
| kya キャ | kyu キュ | kyo キョ | gya ギャ | gyu ギュ | gyo ギョ |
| sha シャ | shu シュ | sho ショ | ja ジャ | ju ジュ | jo ジョ |
| cha チャ | chu チュ | cho チョ | | | |
| nya ニャ | nyu ニュ | nyo ニョ | | | |
| hya ヒャ | hyu ヒュ | hyo ヒョ | | | |
| mya ミャ | myu ミュ | myo ミョ | bya ビャ | byu ビュ | byo ビョ |
| rya リャ | ryu リュ | ryo リョ | pya ピャ | pyu ピュ | pyo ピョ |

Trace the light gray characters, and then try to complete the example words with the correct combined characters.

**kya**   **kyu**   **kyo***

***kyo** キョ is only used in less common words, which are not included here.

1. **kya n pu** (camp)

2. **su kya nā** (scanner)

3. **bā be kyū** (barbecue)

**gya**          **gyu**          **gyo**

4. **gya ra ri i** (gallery)

5. **gya n bu ru** (to gamble; gambling)

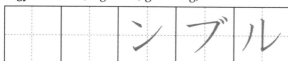

6. **re gyu rā** (regular (gasoline))

7. **gyō za** (pot stickers)

**sha**

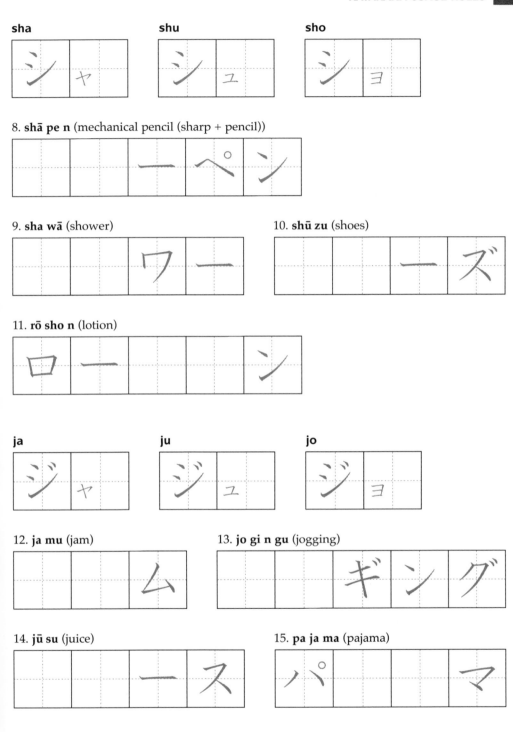

**shu**

**sho**

8. **shā pe n** (mechanical pencil (sharp + pencil))

9. **sha wā** (shower)

10. **shū zu** (shoes)

11. **rō sho n** (lotion)

**ja**

**ju**

**jo**

12. **ja mu** (jam)

13. **jo gi n gu** (jogging)

14. **jū su** (juice)

15. **pa ja ma** (pajama)

**cha**

**chu**

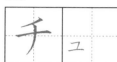

**cho**

16. **cha n ne ru** (channel)

17. **shi chū** (stew)

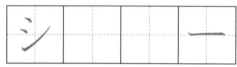

18. **cho ko rē to** (chocolate)

19. **chō ku** (chalk)

**nya\***

**nyu**

**nyo\***

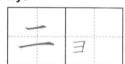

*nya ニャ and **nyo** ニョ are only used in less common words, which are not included here.

20. **me nyū** (menu)

21. **nyū su** (news)

**hya***

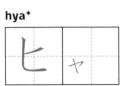

**hyu***

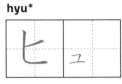

**hyo***

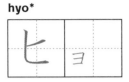

*These character combinations are only used in less common words, which are not included here.

**bya***

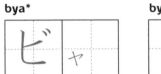

**byu**

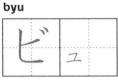

**byo***

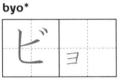

*bya ビャ and byo ビョ are only used in less common words, which are not included here.

22. **i n ta byū** (interview)

23. **re byū** (review)

**pya***

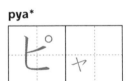

**pyù**

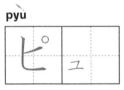

**pyo***

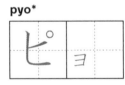

*pya ピャ and pyo ピョ are only used in less common words, which are not included here.

24. **ko n pyū tā** (computer)

25. **pyū ma** (puma)

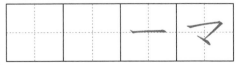

**mya\*** **myu** **myo\***

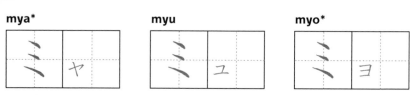

\***mya** ミャ and **myo** ミョ are only used in less common words, which are not included here.

### 26. **myū ji ka ru** (musical)

### 27. **myū to** (mute – volume)

**rya\*** **ryu** **ryo\***

 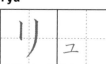 

\***rya** リャ and **ryo** リョ are only used in less common words, which are not included here.

### 28. **ba ryū** (value)

### 29. **bo ryū mu** (volume)

## READING PRACTICE 5: COMBINED CHARACTERS

You should be able to read the words below now. Try covering the answers on the right hand side and reading the katakana words on the left. Try to guess the English meaning of each word before looking at the answers.

キャンプ **kya n pu** (to camp; camping)
スキャナー **su kya nā** (scanner)
バーベキュー **bā be kyū** (barbecue)
ギャラリー **gya ra ri i** (gallery)
レギュラー **re gyu rā** (regular)
ギョーザ **gyō za** (pot stickers)
シャワー **sha wā** (shower)
シューズ **shū zu** (shoes)
ローション **rō sho n** (lotion)
ジャム **ja mu** (jam)
ジャズ **ja zu** (jazz)
ジュース **jū su** (juice)
ジョギング **jo gi n gu** (jogging)
チャンネル **cha n ne ru** (channel)
シチュー **shi chū** (stew)
チョコレート **cho ko rē to** (chocolate)
チョーク **chō ku** (chalk)
メニュー **me nyū** (menu)
ニュース **nyū su** (news)
インタビュー **i n ta byū** (interview)
コンピュータ **ko n pyū tā** (computer)
ミュージカル **myū ji ka ru** (musical)
バリュー **ba ryū** (value)

## RULE 3  SMALL "TSU" ( ッ )

A small **"tsu"** (ッ) is pronounced as a short, silent pause. In romaji it is usually indicated by doubling the following consonant (see examples below). Small **"tsu"** is written in the bottom left hand corner, like small **"ya," "yu"** and **"yo."** Complete the example words by tracing the light gray characters and writing a small **"tsu"** in the appropriate area of the blank boxes.

Example of regular-sized **"tsu"**

Example of small **"tsu"**

1. **ba ggu** (bag)

2. **so kku su** (socks)

3. **pi ku ni kku** (picnic)

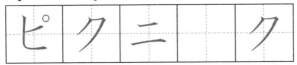

4. **sa kkā** (soccer)

5. **sa n do i cchi** (sandwich)

6. **ki cchi n** (kitchen)

7. **ho tto do ggu** (hotdog)

8. **chi ke tto** (ticket)

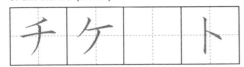

9. **pa i na ppu ru** (pineapple)

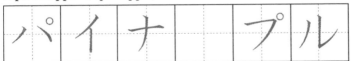

10. **ka ppu** (cup)

# READING PRACTICE 6: SMALL "tsu" ( ッ )

You should be able to read the words below now. Try covering the answers on the right hand side and reading the katakana words on the left. Remember that a small "**tsu**" ッ is read as a short, silent pause. Try to guess the English meaning of each word before looking at the answers.

|  |  |
|---|---|
| ジャケット | **ja ke tto** (jacket) |
| バッグ | **ba ggu** (bag) |
| サンドイッチ | **san n do i cchi** (sandwich) |
| カップ | **ka ppu** (cup) |
| コップ | **ko ppu** (drinking glass) |
| キッチン | **ki cchi n** (kitchen) |
| ベッド | **be ddo** (bed) |
| クローゼット | **ku rō ze tto** (closet) |
| カセットテープ | **ka se tto tē pu** (cassette tape) |
| ペット | **pe tto** (pet) |
| サッカー | **sa kkā** (soccer) |
| クリップ | **ku ri ppu** (paper clip) |
| スケッチ | **su ke cchi** (sketch) |
| キット | **ki tto** (kit) |
| セット | **se tto** (set) |
| ダイエット | **da i e tto** (diet) |
| ポテトチップ | **po te to chi ppu** (potato chips) |
| クラシック | **ku ra shi kku** (classic) |
| コック | **ko kku** (cook) |
| ロッカー | **ro kkā** (locker) |
| ネックレス | **ne kku re su** (necklace) |
| キャッチボール | **kya cchi bō ru** (playing catch) |
| ブレスレット | **bu rē su re tto** (bracelet) |

## RULE 4 — ADDITIONAL COMBINED CHARACTERS

As Japan has become more international, the need to better approximate the foreign names and words from various countries around the world has increased. In 1991 the Japanese government adopted an official list of 32 additional character combinations, and one new character "**vu**" ヴ, for the express purpose of writing foreign words. It also clarified that other additional combinations, as needed, may be used.

You may occasionally see new character combinations as you read books, magazines and web pages. Don't be alarmed, all character combinations follow the same basic principles of pronunciation: the first character indicates the initial sound and it combines with the whole sound of the second character. For example, トゥ takes the initial sound "t" and the final sound "u" to make "**tu**." Since many of the new character combinations are used to write words of foreign languages other than English, and because these words are uncommon in Japanese, the character combination will be introduced, but the unusual examples will not.

**ye***

*ye イエ is only used in less common words, which are not included here.

**wi**

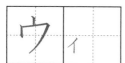

1. **ha ro wi i n** (Halloween)

**we**

2. **we bu** (world wide web)

3. **ku wē to** (Kuwait)

**wo**

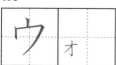

4. **su to ppu wo cchi** (stopwatch)

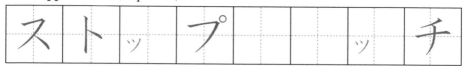

**va**

5. **va i o ri n** (violin, also written バイオリン **ba i o ri n**)

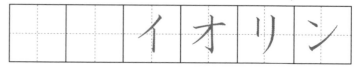

**vi**

6. **vi sa** (visa, also ビサ **bi sa**)

**vu\***

\*vu ヴ is only used in less common words, which are not included here. Perhaps the main purpose of **vu** ヴ is writing the additional character combinations **va** ヴァ, **vi** ヴィ, **ve** ヴェ, **vo** ヴォ.

**ve**

7. **ve to na mu** (vietnam)

**vo**

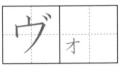

8. **vo ryū mu** (volume, also written ボリューム **bo ryū mu**)

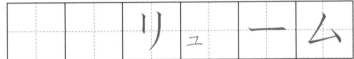

**vyu\***

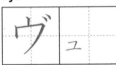

\*vyu ヴュ is only used in less common words, which are not included here.

**kwa\***

\*kwa クァ is only used in less common words, which are not included here.

**kwi\***

\*kwi クィ is only used in less common words, which are not included here.

**kwe\***

\*kwe クェ is only used in less common words, which are not included here.

**kwo**

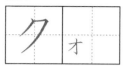

### 9. kwō tē sho n mā ku (quotation marks)

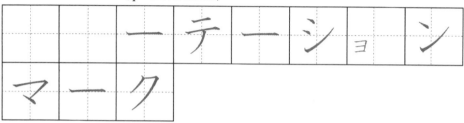

**gwa***

*gwa グァ is only used in less common words, which are not included here.

**she**

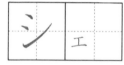

### 10. she fu (chef)

### 11. shē bā (electric shaver)

**je**

### 12. je tto ki* (jet airliner)

*ki would be written in kanji.

**tsa***

*tsa ツァ is only used in less common words, which are not included here.

**tsi***

*tsi* ツィ is only used in less common words, which are not included here.

**tse***

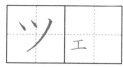

*tse* ツェ is only used in less common words, which are not included here.

**tso***

*tso* ツォ is only used in less common words, which are not included here.

**che**

13. **che su** (chess)

14. **che kku** (check; to check)

**ti**

15. **pā ti i** (party)

**di**

16. **kya n di i** (candy)

**tyu***

*tyu* テュ is only used in less common words, which are not included here.

**dyu**

17. **dyu e tto** (duet)

**tu**

18. **ta tū** (tattoo)

**du***

*du ドゥ is only used in less common words, which are not included here.

**fa**

19. **so fa** (sofa)

20. **fa kku su** (fax)

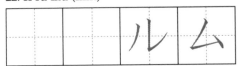

**fi**

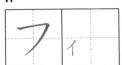

21. **sā fi n** (to surf; surfing)

22. **fi ru mu** (film)

**fe**

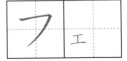

23. **ka fe** (café)

24. **ka fe te ri a** (cafeteria)

**fo**

25. **fo ru dā** (folder)

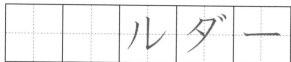

26. **fō ku** (fork)

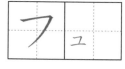

**fyu\***

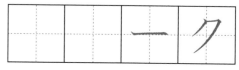

\***fyu** フュ is only used in less common words, which are not included here.

# READING PRACTICE 7: ADDITIONAL COMBINED CHARACTERS

You should be able to read the words below now. Try covering the answers on the right hand side and reading the katakana words on the left. Try to guess the English meaning of each word before looking at the answers.

| | |
|---|---|
| ハ ロ ウ ィ ー ン | **ha ro wi i n** (Halloween) |
| ウ ェ ブ | **we bu** (world wide web) |
| ウ ォ ー ク マ ン | **wō ku ma n** (Walkman) |
| ヴ ァ イ オ リ ン | **va i o ri n** (violin) |
| ヴ ィ サ | **vi sa** (visa) |
| ヴ ェ ト ナ ム | **ve to na mu** (Vietnam) |
| ク ォ ー テ ー シ ョ ン マ ー ク | **kwō te sho n mā ku** (quotation marks) |
| ス ト ッ プ ウ ォ ッ チ | **su to ppu wo cchi** (stopwatch) |
| タ ト ゥ ー | **ta tū** (tattoo) |
| シ ェ フ | **she fu** (chef) |
| ジ ェ ッ ト コ ー ス タ ー | **je tto kō su tā** (rollercoaster) |
| チ ェ ス | **che su** (chess) |
| ス パ ゲ ッ テ ィ | **su pa ge tti** (spaghetti) |
| テ ィ ッ シ ュ | **ti sshu** (tissue) |
| シ ー デ ィ ー | **shi i di i** (CD) |
| デ ュ エ ッ ト | **du e tto** (duet) |
| ソ フ ァ | **so fa** (sofa) |
| サ ー フ ィ ン | **sā fi n** (to surf; surfing) |
| カ フ ェ テ リ ア | **ka fe te ri a** (cafeteria) |
| フ ォ ル ダ ー | **fo ru dā** (folder) |
| フ ォ ー ク | **fō ku** (fork) |

## SECTION SIX
# Reading and Writing Practice

Commonly Mistaken Katakana

Commonly Mistaken Combined Characters

In My Home

Family Restaurant (Food, Part A)

Picnic Lunch (Food, Part B)

Computers and Technology

Sports and Athletics

Sound Symbolic Words

World Map: Africa

World Map: Asia and the Middle East

World Map: Europe

World Map: North and South America

World Map: Oceania

なまえ _____

# Commonly Mistaken Katakana

**Part A:**
Circle the correct katakana character.

| | a | マ ワ ヤ (ア) ケ ヌ フ |
|---|---|---|
| 1. | ko | ヒ コ ロ ヨ ク タ ワ |
| 2. | na | ト ノ イ ネ キ ナ メ |
| 3. | nu | タ ノ ナ ヌ メ ク ケ |
| 4. | su | ヌ ネ ス ク タ メ ヲ |
| 5. | tsu | シ ソ ン リ ツ サ ミ |
| 6. | so | リ ン シ ツ サ メ ソ |
| 7. | te | ニ テ チ メ ヲ ナ ミ |
| 8. | u | ク ワ ヌ フ ラ ウ ヲ |
| 9. | ku | ケ ヲ ク ウ タ ヲ ワ |
| 10. | ni | テ ニ ユ ナ ヲ ミ ヨ |
| 11. | to | ナ イ ノ リ テ オ ト |
| 12. | shi | ツ ソ ン シ リ サ レ |
| 13. | chi | テ オ チ イ ホ ナ ム |
| 14. | ke | ケ ワ フ ク タ ヲ マ |
| 15. | sa | リ シ ツ ン ソ サ ル |
| 16. | ka | ヤ フ ラ カ タ ク ケ |
| 17. | ta | タ ヌ ク ワ ヲ ラ メ |

**Part B:**
Circle the correct katakana character.

| | ho | ハ オ モ ネ (ホ) サ ナ |
|---|---|---|
| 1. | no | タ ク メ ノ ナ ソン |
| 2. | mu | マ ヒ モ ス ワ ム フ |
| 3. | ri | ソ リ ル シ ハン ホ |
| 4. | mo | ヒ セ ニ ミ シ サ モ |
| 5. | ne | フ ネ ラ ホ ハ ウ ラ |
| 6. | ha | ル リ ハ ソ ホ ニ ム |
| 7. | yo | コ ユ ヲ ラ ヨ ワ ニ |
| 8. | ro | コ ヒ モ ロ ヨ ニ エ |
| 9. | ya | ヤ カ マ メ ム メ ヌ |
| 10. | me | ノ ナ メ ヌ タ ク ケ |
| 11. | hi | エ セ ム ヨ コ モ ヒ |
| 12. | ru | レ リ ル ハ ニ ノ ナ |
| 13. | ma | ム ア ウ マ ヌ メ ク |
| 14. | mi | ニ ミ ツ ン ソ キ シ |
| 15. | ra | テ ラ ウ モ フ ワ ヲ |
| 16. | fu | ク ワ ヲ ケ フ タ ナ |
| 17. | yu | コ ヨ ラ ワ ニ ヲ ユ |

Time _____:_____          Time _____:_____

なまえ ＿＿＿＿＿＿＿＿＿＿

# Commonly Mistaken Combined Characters

**Part A:**
Circle the correct combined character.

| ju | シュ | ジョ | (ジュ) | ショ |
|---|---|---|---|---|
| 1. **gya** | ギャ | キャ | ギュ | キュ |
| 2. **sha** | シュ | ショ | ジョ | シャ |
| 3. **nyo** | ミョ | ニョ | ニャ | ミュ |
| 4. **myu** | ミョ | ニュ | ミュ | ミャ |
| 5. **jo** | ショ | ジュ | シュ | ジョ |
| 6. **pyu** | ピャ | ピュ | ヒュ | ピョ |
| 7. **kyo** | キャ | ギャ | キョ | ギョ |
| 8. **chu** | チャ | チュ | ショ | シュ |
| 9. **bya** | ビャ | ヒャ | ピャ | ビュ |
| 10. **hya** | ヒュ | ヒャ | ピャ | ビャ |
| 11. **ryo** | リュ | ジュ | ニョ | リョ |
| 12. **kya** | ギャ | キュ | キャ | ギョ |
| 13. **byo** | ピョ | ヒュ | ビョ | ヒョ |
| 14. **gyo** | キョ | ギュ | ギャ | ギョ |
| 15. **ryu** | リュ | リョ | ニュ | リャ |

**Part B:**
Circle the correct combined character.

| di* | ティ | テュ | デュ | (ディ) |
|---|---|---|---|---|
| 1. **wi** | ヴィ | ウィ | ウェ | ウォ |
| 2. **du*** | トゥ | テュ | ドゥ | デュ |
| 3. **fo** | フィ | フェ | ファ | フォ |
| 4. **vo** | ヴォ | ウォ | ヴュ | ヴィ |
| 5. **qwo*** | グォ | クァ | クォ | クィ |
| 6. **va** | ウィ | ヴァ | ヴェ | ヴィ |
| 7. **ti*** | ディ | デュ | テュ | ティ |
| 8. **tu*** | ドゥ | トゥ | テュ | ティ |
| 9. **je** | ジェ | シェ | チェ | クェ |
| 10. **qwa*** | ジャ | ファ | ツァ | クァ |
| 11. **ve** | ウェ | ヴェ | クェ | シェ |
| 12. **gwa*** | クァ | ファ | グァ | ヴァ |
| 13. **ye** | クェ | イェ | ヴェ | ツェ |
| 14. **dyu*** | デュ | ヴュ | ツァ | ツォ |
| 15. **che** | ウェ | フェ | チェ | ヴェ |

*These spellings indicate the pronunciation. When typing, however, the "x" key is used to type small characters, rather than using these spellings.

Time ＿＿＿:＿＿＿     Time ＿＿＿:＿＿＿

なまえ _____

## In My Home

**Part A:** Label the places in this home with katakana characters.

1. bedroom (**be ddo rū mu**)
⬜⬜⬜⬜⬜⬜

2. shower (**sha wā**)
⬜⬜⬜⬜

3. toilet, restroom (**to i re**)
⬜⬜⬜

4. living room (**ri bi n gu rū mu**)
⬜⬜⬜⬜⬜⬜⬜

5. dining room (**da i ni n gu rū mu**)
⬜⬜⬜⬜⬜⬜⬜⬜

6. kitchen (**ki cchi n**)
⬜⬜⬜⬜

**Part B:** Complete the sentences below by describing where each household item is located.

1. The blender (**mi ki sā**) is in the kitchen.
ミキサーは　キッチンに　あります。

2. The sofa (**so fa**) is in the living room.
_____。

3. The slippers (**su ri ppā**) are in the restroom.
_____。

4. The microwave (*de n shi** **re n ji*) is in the kitchen.
でんし_____ は _____に　あります。

5. The sewing machine (**mi shi n**) is in the closet (**ku rō ze tto**).
_____。

6. The desk lamp (*de n ki** **su ta n do*) is in the bedroom.
でんき_____。

7. The table (**tē bu ru**) is in the dining room.
_____。

8. The iron (**a i ro n**) is in the closet (**ku rō ze tto**).
_____。

*hiragana

なまえ _____

# Family Restaurant (Food, Part A)

menu (**me nyū**)

1. sandwich (**sa n do i cchi**)
¥400

2. cheese pizza (**chi i zu pi za**)
¥400

3. hamburger (**ha n bā gā**)
¥450

4. hotdog (**ho tto do ggu**)
¥350

5. spaghetti (**su pa ge tti**)
¥550

6. ramen noodles (**rā me n**)
¥400

7. curry rice (**ka rē ra i su**)
¥550

8. hamburger steak (**ha n bā gu**)
¥750

9. steak (**su tē ki**)
¥950

10. French fries (**po te to fu ra i**)
¥350

11. salad (**sa ra da**)
¥400

12. soup (**sū pu**)
¥350

13. melon soda float (**ku ri i mu sō da**)
¥400

14. tomato juice (**to ma to jū su**)
¥300

15. orange juice (**o re n ji jū su**)
¥300

16. cola (**kō ra**)
¥350

17. milk (**mi ru ku**)
¥300

18. coffee (**kō hi i**)
¥350

19. ice tea (**a i su ti i**)
¥350

20. pudding (**pu ri n**)
¥350

21. ice cream (**a i su ku ri i mu**)
¥350

22. sherbet (**shā be tto**)
¥350

23. cheese cake (**chi i zu kē ki**)
¥400

なまえ _____

# Picnic Lunch (Food, Part B)

Taro has almost finished packing a picnic lunch.
He wants a few more fruits, snacks, utensils and condiments.
Write in katakana below the choices he could consider.

1. oranges (**o re n ji**)

2. bananas (**ba na na**)

3. melon (**me ro n**)

4. pineapple (**pa i na ppu ru**)

5. mango (**ma n gō**)

6. kiwi fruit (**ki u i fu rū tsu**)

7. grapefruit (**gu rē pu fu rū tsu**)

8. cherries (**che ri i**)

9. olives (**o ri i bu**)

10. avocado (**a bo ka do**)

11. tomato (**to ma to**)

12. lettuce (**re ta su**)

13. celery (**se ro ri**)

14. peanuts (**pi i na ttsu**)

15. potato chips (**po te to chi ppu su**)

16. cookies (**ku kki i**)

17. crackers (**ku ra kkā**)

18. candy (**kya n di i**)

19. chocolate (**cho ko rē to**)

20. gum (**ga mu**)

21. popsicles (**a i su kya n di i**)

22. cheese (**chi i zu**)

23. yogurt (**yō gu ru to**)

24. salad dressing (**do re sshi n gu**)

25. ketchup (**ke cha ppu**)

なまえ _____

# Computers and Technology

1. computer (**ko n pyū tā**)

2. personal computer (**pa so ko n**)

3. notebook computer (**nō to pa so ko n**)

4. mouse (**ma u su**)

5. keyboard (**ki i bō do**)

6. monitor (**mo ni tā**)

7. printer (**pu ri n tā**)

8. software (**so fu to**)*

9. modem (**mo de mu**)

10. web (**we bu**)

11. internet (**i n tā ne tto**)

12. home page (**hō mu pē ji**)

13. email (**mē ru**)*

14. camera (**ka me ra**)

15. digital camera (**de ji ka me**)*

16. video camera (**bi de o ka me ra**)

17. lens (**re n zu**)

18. film (**fi ru mu**)

19. TV; television (**te re bi**)

20. remote control (**ri mo ko n**)

21. video tape (**bi de o tē pu**)

22. DVD player (**DVD pu rē yā**)

| D | V | D | | | | |
|---|---|---|---|---|---|---|

23. MP3 player (**MP3 pu rē yā**)

| M | P | 3 | | | | |
|---|---|---|---|---|---|---|

24. earphones (**i ya ho n**)

25. radio (**ra ji o**)

26. cell phone (**kē ta i**)**

---

* Although commonly abbreviated, "software" is also written ソフトウェア (**so fu to we a**); "email" is also 電子
メール (**de n shi mē ru**) or イーメール (**i i mē ru**); "digital camera" is also デジタルカメラ (**de ji ta ru ka me ra**).
** "Cell phone" is commonly written in katakana, but is still officially written in kanji 携帯電話 (**ke i ta i de n wa**).

なまえ _____

## Sports and Athletics

1. sports (**su pō tsu**)

2. Olympics (**o ri n pi kku**)

3. basketball (**ba su ke tto bō ru**)

4. volleyball (**ba rē bō ru**)

5. golf (**go ru fu**)

6. football (**a me fu to**)*

7. lacrosse (**ra ku ro su**)

8. tennis (**te ni su**)

9. rugby (**ra gu bi i**)

10. soccer (**sa kkā**)

11. score (**su ko a**)

12. goal (**gō ru**)

13. team (**chi i mu**)

14. uniform (**yu ni fō mu**)

15. skiing (**su ki i**)

16. snowboarding (**su nō bō do**)

17. ice skating (**a i su su kē to**)

18. ice hockey (**a i su ho kkē**)

19. surfing (**sā fi n**)

20. diving (**da i bi n gu**)

21. skateboarding (**su ke bō**)*

22. wrestling (**re su ri n gu**)

23. boxing (**bo ku shi n gu**)

24. taekwondo (**te ko n dō**)

25. marathon (**ma ra so n**)

---

\* Although commonly abbreviated, "(American) football" is also written アメリカンフットボール (**a me ri ka n fu tto bō ru**); "skateboarding" is also written スケートボード (**su kē to bō do**).

なまえ _____

# Sound Symbolic Words

## General Sounds

1. The rain is pouring down.
   あめが（　　）ふっている。　　**(zā zā)**
2. The wind is howling.
   かぜが（　　）と ふいている。　**(hyū hyū)**
3. The phone is ringing.
   でんわが（　　）と なっている。　**(ri i n)**
4. The microwave timer rang.
   でんしレンジが（　　）と なった。　**(chi n)**
5. The children made a lot of noise.
   こどもが（　　）さわいだ。　　**(wa i wa i)**

## Animal Sounds

6. Dogs say "Woof! Woof!"
   いぬは（　　）と なく。　　**(wan wan)**
7. Cats say "meow."
   ねこは（　　）と なく。　　**(nyā)**
8. Crows say "kah kah."
   カラスは（　　）と なく。　　**(kā kā)**
9. Frogs say "ribbit."
   かえるは（　　）と なく。　　**(ke ro ke ro)**
10. Mice say "squeak!"
    ねずみは（　　）と なく。　　**(chū chū)**
11. Roosters say "cock-a-doodle-doo!"
    にわとりは（　　）と なく。　　**(ko ke ko kkō)**

## Psychological States

12. I'm excited (nervous/anxious; lit. my heart is pounding).
    むねが（　　）する。　　**(do ki do ki)**
13. I'm excited (positive sense; lit. my heart is fluttering).
    むねが（　　）する。　　**(wa ku wa ku)**

ニャー

なまえ ＿＿＿＿＿＿＿＿＿＿＿＿

# World Map: Africa

1. Algeria (**a ru je ri a**)

2. Angola (**a n go ra**)

3. Uganda (**u ga n da**)

4. Egypt (**e ji pu to**)

5. Ethiopia (**e chi o pi a**)

6. Eritrea (**e ri to ri a**)

7. Ghana (**gā na**)

8. Cape Verde (**kā bo be ru de**)

9. Canary Islands (**ka na ri a sho tō**)*
諸島

10. Gabon (**ga bo n**)

11. Cameroon (**ka me rū n**)

12. Gambia (**ga n bi a**)

13. Guinea (**gi ni a**)

14. Guinea-Bissau (**gi ni a bi sa u**)

15. Ivory Coast (**kō to ji bo wā ru**)

16. Sao Tome and Principe (**sa n to me pu ri n shi pu**)

17. Republic of the Congo (**ko n go** *kyō wa ko ku*)*
共和国

18. Democratic Republic of the Congo (**ko n go** *mi n shu kyō wa ko ku*)*
民主共和国

19. Kenya (**ke ni a**)

20. Comoros (**ko mo ro**)

21. Zambia (**za n bi a**)

22. Sierra Leone (**she ra re o ne**)

23. Djibouti (**ji bu chi**)

24. Zimbabwe (**ji n ba bu e**)

25. Sudan (**sū da n**)

26. Swaziland (**su wa ji ra n do**)

27. Seychelles (**se i she ru**)

28. Equatorial Guinea (*se ki dō* **gi ni a**)*
赤道

29. Senegal (**se ne ga ru**)

30. Somali (**so ma ri a**)

31. Tanzania (**ta n za ni a**)

32. Chad (**cha do**)

33. Tunisia (**chu ni ji a**)

34. Togo (**tō go**)

35. Nigeria (**na i je ri a**)

36. Namibia (**na mi bi a**)

37. Niger (**ni jē ru**)

38. Central African Republic (*chū ō a fu ri ka*)*
中央

39. Western Sahara (*ni shi* **sa ha ra**)*
西

40. Burkina Faso (**bu ru ki na fa so**)

41. Burundi (**bu ru n ji**)

42. Benin (**be na n**)

43. Botswana (**bo tsu wa na**)

44. Madagascar (**ma da ga su ka ru**)

45. Malawi (**ma ra u i**)

46. Mali (**ma ri**)

47. Mauritius (**mō ri sha su**)

48. Mauritania (**mō ri ta ni a**)

49. Mozambique (**mo za n bi i ku**)

50. Morocco (**mo ro kko**)

51. Libya (**ri bi a**)

52. Liberia (**ri be ri a**)

53. Rwanda (**ru wa n da**)

54. Lesotho (**re so to**)

55. Reunion (**re yu ni o n**)

56. South Africa (*mi na mi* **a fu ri ka**)*
南

* *Italic* letters indicate the kanji pronunciation.

なまえ ＿＿＿＿＿＿＿＿＿＿＿

# World Map: Asia and the Middle East

(In Asia most country names are written in katakana, except for Japan 日本; North Korea 北朝鮮; South Korea 韓国; China 中国 and Taiwan 台湾.)

1. Cyprus (**ki pu ro su**)

2. Lebanon (**re ba no n**)

3. Palestine (**pa re su chi na**)

4. Israel (**i su ra e ru**)

5. Jordan (**yo ru da n**)

6. Mongolia (**mo n go ru**)

7. Macao (**ma ka o**)

8. Philippines (**fi ri pi n**)

9. Vietnam (**be to na mu**)

10. Laos (**ra o su**)

11. Cambodia (**ka n bo ji a**)

12. Brunei (**bu ru ne i**)

13. Malaysia (**ma rē shi a**)

14. Singapore (**shi n ga pō ru**)

15. Indonesia (**i n do ne shi a**)

16. Thailand (**ta i**)

17. Myanmar (**mya n mā**)

18. Bangladesh (**ba n gu ra de shu**)

19. Bhutan (**bū ta n**)

20. Nepal (**ne pā ru**)

21. India (**i n do**)

22. Sri Lanka (**su ri ra n ka**)

23. Maldives (**mo ru di vu**)

24. Pakistan (**pa ki su ta n**)

25. Afghanistan (**a fu ga ni su ta n**)

26. Iran (**i ra n**)

27. Tajikistan (**ta ji ki su ta n**)

28. Kyrgyz (**ki ru gi su**)

29. Kazakhstan (**ka za fu su ta n**)

30. Uzbekistan (**u zu be ki su ta n**)

31. Turkmenistan (**to ru ku me ni su ta n**)

32. Azerbaijan (**a ze ru ba i ja n**)

33. Georgia (**gu ru ji a**)

34. Turkey (**to ru ko**)

35. Armenia (**a ru me ni a**)

36. Syria (**shi ri a**)

37. Iraq (**i ra ku**)

38. Saudi Arabia (**sa u ji a ra bi a**)

39. Oman (**o mā n**)

40. Yemen (**i e me n**)

41. UAE* (**a ra bu** *shu chō koku ren pō*)

首 長 国 連 邦

* (United Arab Emirates, *italic* letters indicate the kanji pronunciation.)

なまえ _____

# World Map: Europe

1. Iceland (**a i su ra n do**)

2. Ireland (**a i ru ra n do**)

3. Albania (**a ru ba ni a**)

4. Andorra (**a n do ra**)

5. England (**i gi ri su**)

6. Italy (**i ta ri a**)

7. Ukraine (**u ku ra i na**)

8. Estonia (**e su to ni a**)

9. Austria (**ō su to ri a**)

10. Holland (**o ra n da**)

11. Greece (**gi ri sha**)

12. Croatia (**ku ro a chi a**)

13. San Marino (**sa n ma ri no**)

14. Gibraltar (**gi bu ra ru ta ru**)

15. Switzerland (**su i su**)

16. Sweden (**su wē de n**)

17. Spain (**su pe i n**)

18. Slovakia (**su ro ba ki a**)

19. Slovenia (**su ro be ni a**)

20. Czech Republic (**che ko**)

21. Denmark (**de n mā ku**)

22. Germany (**do i tsu**)

23. Norway (**no ru wē**)

24. Vatican City (**ba chi ka n**)  市 国

25. Hungary (**ha n ga ri i**)

26. Finland (**fi n ra n do**)

27. Faroe Islands (**fe rō *sho tō***)*  諸 島

28. France (**fu ra n su**)

29. Russia (**ro shi a**)

30. Bulgaria (**bu ru ga ri a**)

31. Belarus (**be ra rū shi**)

32. Belgium (**be ru gi i**)

33. Poland (**pō ra n do**)

34. Portugal (**po ru to ga ru**)

35. Macedonia (**ma ke do ni a**)

36. Malta (**ma ru ta**)

37. Serbia and Montenegro (**se ru bi a • mo n te ne gu ro**)

38. Monaco (**mo na ko**)

39. Moldova (**mo ru do ba**)

40. Latvia (**ra to bi a**)

41. Lithuania (**ri to a ni a**)

42. Liechtenstein (**ri hi te n shu ta i n**)

43. Romania (**rū ma ni a**)

44. Luxembourg (**ru ku se n bu ru ku**)

45. Bosnia and Herzegovina (**bo su ni a • he ru tse go bi na**)

* *Italic* letters indicate the kanji pronunciation.

なまえ ＿＿＿＿＿＿＿＿＿

# World Map: North and South America

1. Greenland (**gu ri i n ra n do**)

2. Canada (**ka na da**)

3. United State of America
(**a me ri ka** *ga sshū koku*)*

合 衆 国

4. Mexico (**me ki shi ko**)

5. Guatemala (**gu a te ma ra**)

6. Belize (**be ri i zu**)

7. El Salvador (**e ru sa ru ba do ru**)

8. Honduras (**ho n ju ra su**)

9. Nicaragua (**ni ka ra gu a**)

10. Costa Rica (**ko su ta ri ka**)

11. Panama
(**pa na ma**)

12. Bermuda Islands (**ba myū da**)

13. The Bahamas (**ba ha ma**)

14. Cuba (**kyū ba**)

15. Venezuela (**be ne zu e ra**)

16. Colombia (**ko ro n bi a**)

17. Ecuador (**e ku a do ru**)

18. Guyana (**ga i a na**)

19. Suriname (**su ri na mu**)

20. French Guiana (**fu ra n su** *ryō* **gi a na**)*

領

21. Peru (**pe rū**)

22. Brazil (**bu ra ji ru**)

23. Bolivia (**bo ri bi a**)

24. Paraguay (**pa ra gu a i**)

25. Chile (**chi ri**)

26. Argentina (**a ru ze n chi n**)

27. Uruguay (**u ru gu a i**)

28. Falkland Islands (**fō ku ra n do** *sho tō*)*

諸 島

* *Italic* letters indicate the kanji pronunciation.

なまえ _____

# World Map: Oceania

1. American Samoa
(**a me ri ka** *ryō* **sa mo a**)*

| | | | 領 | | | |
|---|---|---|---|---|---|---|

2. Australia (**ō su to ra ri a**)

| | | | | | | |
|---|---|---|---|---|---|---|

3. Northern Mariana Islands
(*ki ta* **ma ri a na** *sho tō*)*

| 北 | | | | | 諸 | 島 |
|---|---|---|---|---|---|---|

4. Kiribati (**ki ri ba su**)

| き | | | す |
|---|---|---|---|

5. Guam (**gu a mu**)

| | あ | |
|---|---|---|

6. Cook Islands (**ku kku** *sho tō*)*

| く | | | 諸 | 島 |
|---|---|---|---|---|

7. Samoa (**sa mo a**)

| さ | | あ |
|---|---|---|

8. Solomon Islands (**so ro mo n** *sho tō*)*

| そ | | | え | 諸 | 島 |
|---|---|---|---|---|---|

9. Tuvalu (**tsu ba ru**)

| つ | | |
|---|---|---|

10. Tonga (**to n ga**)

| | | |
|---|---|---|

11. Nauru (**na u ru**)

| | | |
|---|---|---|

12. New Caledonia (**nyū ka re do ni a**)

| | | | | | | |
|---|---|---|---|---|---|---|

13. New Zealand (**nyū ji i ra n do**)

| | | | | | |
|---|---|---|---|---|---|

14. Vanuatu (**ba nu a tsu**)

| | | | |
|---|---|---|---|

15. Papua New Guinea (**pa pu a nyū gi ni a**)

| | | | | | | |
|---|---|---|---|---|---|---|

16. Palau (**pa ra o**)

| | | |
|---|---|---|

17. Fiji (**fi ji i**)

| | | |
|---|---|---|

18. Marshall Islands (**mā sha ru** *sho tō*)*

| | | | | 諸 | 島 |
|---|---|---|---|---|---|

19. Micronesia (**mi ku ro ne shi a**)

| | | | | | |
|---|---|---|---|---|---|

20. French Polynesia (**fu ra n su** *ryō* **po ri ne shi a**)*

| | | | | 領 | | | | | |
|---|---|---|---|---|---|---|---|---|---|

*Italic letters indicate the kanji pronunciation.

## Answers

**Commonly Mistaken Katakana (page 174)** **Part A** 1. コ  2. ナ  3. ヌ  4. ス  5. ツ  6. ソ  7. テ  8. ウ  9. ク  10. ニ  11. ト  12. シ  13. チ  14. ケ  15. サ  16. カ  17. タ  **Part B** 1. ノ  2. ム  3. リ  4. モ  5. ネ  6. ハ  7. ヨ  8. ロ  9. ヤ  10. メ  11. ヒ  12. ル  13. マ  14. ミ  15. ラ  16. フ  17. ユ

**Commonly Mistaken Combined Characters (page 175)** **Part A** 1. ギャ  2. シャ  3. ニョ  4. ミュ  5. ジョ  6. ピュ  7. キョ  8. チュ  9. ビャ  10. ヒャ  11. リョ  12. キャ  13. ビョ  14. ギョ  15. リュ  **Part B** 1. ウィ  2. ドゥ  3. フォ  4. ヴォ  5. クォ  6. ヴァ  7. ティ  8. トゥ  9. ジェ  10. クァ  11. ヴェ  12. グァ  13. イェ  14. デュ  15. チェ

**In My Home (page 176)** **Part A** 1. ベッドルーム  2. シャワー  3. トイレ  4. リビングルーム  5. ダイニングルーム  6. キッチン  **Part B** 2. ソファ、リビングルーム  3. スリッパ、トイレ  4. レンジ、キッチン  5. ミシン、クローゼット  6. スタンド、ベッドルーム  7. テーブル、ダイニングルーム  8. アイロン、クローゼット

**Family Restaurant (Food, Part A) (page 177)** メニュー  1. サンドイッチ  2. チーズピザ  3. ハンバーガー  4. ホットドッグ  5. スパゲッティ  6. ラーメン  7. カレーライス  8. ハンバーグ  9. ステーキ  10. ポテトフライ  11. サラダ  12. スープ  13. クリームソーダ  14. トマトジュース  15. オレンジジュース  16. コーラ  17. ミルク  18. コーヒー  19. アイスティー  20. プリン  21. アイスクリーム  22. シャーベット  23. チーズケーキ

**Picnic Lunch (Food, Part B) (page 178)** 1. オレンジ  2. バナナ  3. メロン  4. パイナップル  5. マンゴー  6. キウイフルーツ  7. グレープフルーツ  8. チェリー  9. オリーブ  10. アボカド  11. トマト  12. レタス  13. セロリ  14. ピーナッツ  15. ポテトチップス  16. クッキー  17. クラッカー  18. キャンディー  19. チョコレート  20. ガム  21. アイスキャンディー  22. チーズ  23. ヨーグルト  24. ドレッシング  25. ケチャップ

**Computers and Technology (page 179)** 1. コンピューター  2. パソコン  3. ノートパソコン  4. マウス  5. キーボード  6. モニター  7. プリンター  8. ソフト  9. モデム  10. ウェブ  11. インターネット  12. ホームページ  13. メール  14. カメラ  15. デジカメ  16. ビデオカメラ  17. レンズ  18. フィルム  19. テレビ  20. リモコン  21. ビデオテープ  22. プレーヤー  23. プレーヤー  24. イヤホン  25. ラジオ  26. ケータイ

**Sports and Athletics (page 180)** 1. スポーツ  2. オリンピック  3. バスケットボール  4. バレーボール  5. ゴルフ  6. アメフト  7. ラクロス  8. テニス  9. ラグビー  10. サッカー  11. スコア  12. ゴール  13. チーム  14. ユニフォーム  15. スキー  16. スノーボード  17. アイススケート  18. アイスホッケー  19. サーフィン  20. ダイビング  21. スケボー  22. レスリング  23. ボクシング  24. テコンドー  25. マラソン

**Sound Symbolic Words (page 181)** 1. ザーザー  2. ヒューヒュー  3. リーン  4. チン  5. ワイワイ  6. ワンワン  7. ニャー  8. カーカー  9. ケロケロ  10. チューチュー  11. コケコッコー  12. ドキドキ  13. ワクワク

**World Map: Africa (page 182)** 1. アルジェリア  2. アンゴラ  3. ウガンダ  4. エジプト  5. エチオピア  6. エリトリア  7. ガーナ  8. カーボベルデ  9. カナリア  10. ガボン  11. カメルーン  12. ガンビア  13. ギニア  14. ギニアビサウ  15. コートジボワール  16. サントメプリンシペ  17. コンゴ  18. コンゴ  19. ケニア  20. コモロ  21. ザンビア  22. シエラレオネ  23. ジブチ  24. ジンバブエ  25. スーダン  26. スワジランド  27. セイシェル  28. ギニア  29. セネガル  30. ソマリア  31. タンザニア  32. チャド  33. チュニジア  34. トーゴ  35. ナイジェリア  36. ナミビア  37. ニジェール  38. アフリカ  39. サハラ  40. ブルキナファソ  41. ブルンジ  42. ベナン  43. ボツワナ  44. マダガスカル  45. マラウイ  46. マリ  47. モーリシャス  48. モーリタニア  49. モザンビーク  50. モロッコ  51. リビア  52. リベリア  53. ルワンダ  54. レソト  55. レユニオン  56. アフリカ

**World Map: Asia and the Middle East (page 183)** 1. キプロス  2. レバノン  3. パレスチナ  4. イスラエル  5. ヨルダン  6. モンゴル  7. マカオ  8. フィリピン  9. ベトナム  10. ラオス  11. カンボジア  12. ブルネイ  13. マレーシア  14. シンガポール  15. インドネシア  16. タイ  17. ミャンマー  18. バングラデシュ  19. ブータン  20. ネパール  21. インド  22. スリランカ  23. モルディヴ  24. パキスタン  25. アフガニスタン  26. イラン  27. タジキスタン  28. キルギス  29. カザフスタン  30. ウズベキスタン  31. トルクメニスタン  32. アゼルバイジャン  33. グルジア  34. トルコ  35. アルメニア  36. シリア  37. イラク  38. サウジアラビア  39. オマーン  40. イエメン  41. アラブ

**World Map: Europe (page 184)** 1. アイスランド  2. アイルランド  3. アルバニア  4. アンドラ  5. イギリス  6. イタリア  7. ウクライナ  8. エストニア  9. オーストリア  10. オランダ  11. ギリシャ  12. クロアチア  13. サンマリノ  14. ジブラルタル  15. スイス  16. スウェーデン  17. スペイン  18. スロバキア  19. スロベニア  20. チェコ  21. デンマーク  22. ドイツ  23. ノルウェー  24. バチカン  25. ハンガリー  26. フィンランド  27. フェロー  28. フランス  29. ロシア  30. ブルガリア  31. ベラルーシ  32. ベルギー  33. ポーランド  34. ポルトガル  35. マケドニア  36. マルタ  37. セルビア・モンテネグロ  38. モナコ  39. モルドバ  40. ラトビア  41. リトアニア  42. リヒテンシュタイン  43. ルーマニア  44. ルクセンブルク  45. ボスニア・ヘルツェゴビナ

**World Map: North America and South America (page 185)** 1. グリーンランド  2. カナダ  3. アメリカ  4. メキシコ  5. グアテマラ  6. ベリーズ  7. エルサルバドル  8. ホンジュラス  9. ニカラグア  10. コスタリカ  11. パナマ  12. バミューダ  13. バハマ  14. キューバ  15. ベネズエラ  16. コロンビア  17. エクアドル  18. ガイアナ  19. スリナム  20. フランス、ギアナ  21. ペルー  22. ブラジル  23. ボリビア  24. パラグアイ  25. チリ  26. アルゼンチン  27. ウルグアイ  28. フォークランド

**World Map: Oceania (page 186)** 1. アメリカ、サモア  2. オーストラリア  3. マリアナ  4. キリバス  5. グアム or グァム  6. クック  7. サモア  8. ソロモン  9. ツバル  10. トンガ  11. ナウル  12. ニューカレドニア  13. ニュージーランド  14. バヌアツ  15. パプアニューギニア  16. パラオ  17. フィジー  18. マーシャル  19. ミクロネシア  20. フランス、ポリネシア

# Flash Card Practice Activities

It is much easier to learn to read hiragana and katakana than to write them. With the right kinds of activities, diligent students can learn to read the basic 46 hiragana in a few hours, and the 46 katakana in another few hours. You will more readily learn the writing once you have mastered hiragana and katakana reading recognition, so it is suggested you begin your learning work with the flash cards.

Start by printing the flash card PDFs out—you may decide to print either the entire 92 cards, or only the group you'll be focusing on first (hiragana or katakana). Print double-sided cards, or print the fronts and backs separately then attach them together. Next, separate the flash cards by cutting along the perforated lines. If you are unfamiliar with hiragana and katakana take the time to read the front and back of each flash card, paying close attention to the number and type of strokes used in each character. Many hiragana characters look similar, and so do many katakana; it is the number and type of strokes that will help to tell them apart.

**Hiragana/Katakana Flash Card Drills** (alone or with a partner): It is helpful to start with a few, perhaps 10, flash cards. Shuffle the flash cards and look at them one at a time. Say the name of the character on the top flash card, then look at the back to see if you got it right. Start two piles of flash cards. If correct, place it in one pile. If not, place it in an another pile, to be reviewed again. Continue looking at the flash cards one at a time and placing them in the appropriate pile. When you are finished, you will know which characters you can read and which ones need more practice. Now put aside the ones you already know and study the flash cards you had difficulty with. When ready, repeat the activity with the difficult ones. As you gain mastery add more flash cards, until you know all 46 hiragana and all 46 katakana. Then, shuffle both groups of cards together to do a challenge round! You can repeat this simple activity from time to time to refresh your basic hiragana and katakana reading skills.

**Hiragana/Katakana Chart Activity** (alone or with a small group): This is an excellent activity to improve your hiragana/katakana recognition skills and become familiar with **gojūon** order—the way dictionaries, web searches, etc., are organized. Place all the flash cards on a large surface (the floor works well) face up, in random order. Then, try to put them into order as quickly as possible. For an extra challenge use a stopwatch.

**Hiragana/Katakana Pick-up** (small group): Place all the flash cards on a large surface face up, in order or mixed up. One person calls the name of a hiragana/katakana character and the other players try to quickly put their hand on it. The first one gets to keep it. Continue playing, and when all the flash cards are gone, count to see who has the most. The winner gets to be the "caller" for the next game!

## Acknowledgments

I am deeply grateful to the many individuals who have contributed valuable comments and suggestions on this book. I am particularly grateful to former colleagues at the American School in Japan: For help especially on hiragana sections, Clark Tenney, Keiko Yasuno, Keiko Ando, Sumino Hirano, Mariko Smisson, Jo Ash, Anita Gesling, Maki Ushigome, Machiko Romaine, Naoko Pennell, and Leslie Birkland; for help especially on katakana sections, Keiko Yasuno, Keiko Ando, Sumino Hirano, Mariko Smisson, Yuko Hayashi, and Clark Tenney. I also wish to thank Noriko Okada (Waterford School) and Shauna Stout for their careful proof-reading and valuable feedback. Many others offered their support, and I wish to sincerely thank Dr. Masakazu Watabe, LaNae Stout, Linda Gerber, Shauna Stout, and Ricky Stout. I also wish to thank the helpful people at Tuttle Publishing.

# The CD-ROM contains these helpful resources:

- 600 Common Names.pdf
  A list of common English female and male first names, with their **katakana** versions.

- Flash Card Practice Activities.pdf

- Printable Flash Cards:
  - for all **hiragana** characters
  - for all **katakana** characters

- Self quiz

- Bonus writing practice pages